ALIVE WITH THE SPIRIT

ALIVE WITH THE SPIRIT

Martin H. Franzmann

Publishing House
St. Louis London

Concordia Publishing House, St. Louis, Missouri
Concordia Publishing House Ltd., London E. C. 1
Copyright © 1973 Concordia Publishing House

ISBN 0-570-03174-5

MANUFACTURED IN THE UNITED STATES OF AMERICA

Contents

Still the Spirit Comes	7
Life and Liberty	9
Not Crawling but Walking	12
The Christian's New Mind-Set	15
Bearing the Mark of Jesus	18
Dying in Order to Live	20
From Fear to Fellowship with Christ	23
The Homecoming Saint	25
Aglow with the Spirit	28
Abounding in Hope	30
Ransomed Bodies	32
The Spirit's Greatest Gift	34
Gifts for the Service of All	37
Wisdom and Knowledge: Choice Gifts	41
Men Alive	43
Reflectors of God's Glory	45
Avoiding What Is Fleshly and Foolish	48
The Fruits of the Spirit	50
The Spirit's Marching Orders	53
The Promise of Power	55
Individuality amid Unity	58
Stamped with the Spirit's Seal	60
Drinking from a Golden Goblet	63
On Wings of Prayer	65
Worship in the Spirit	68
The Spirit and the Flesh	70
Uses of the Spirit's Word	73
Our Guide into All Truth	76
Waiting for the Bridegroom	78

Still the Spirit Comes

And all were amazed and perplexed, saying to one another, "What does this mean?" But others mocking said, "They are filled with new wine." (Acts 2:12-13)

Christmas and Pentecost, the coming of Christ and the coming of the Holy Spirit, present a tragic parallel. The Christ came to His own people, the hoped-for and longed-for Messiah to whom all His people's prophets testified, the Yes to all the promises that God had made to Israel. He came as the Light to a people walking in darkness — and they loved darkness rather than light.

Jesus came to His home city of Nazareth and spoke to His fellow townsmen the gracious words from the Book of Isaiah which proclaim "the acceptable year of the Lord." These words of Isaiah were fulfilled "in their hearing"; as Jesus spoke the ancient promise He by His presence fulfilled the promise. As He spoke, the last great year of jubilee — with its blessing of release from captivity, recovery of sight for the blind, liberty for the oppressed, good news for every need of man — that year of jubilee began. The men of Nazareth marveled at "the gracious words" but doubted whether He who spoke them and announced Himself as their Fulfiller were anything more than the carpenter's Son. And when the carpenter's Son called on them to repent and believe, their wondering skepticism turned to wrath, and they were ready to hurl Him headlong from the brow of the hill on which their city was built.

The Holy Spirit came in fulfilment of the promises of God made through the prophets, through John the Baptist, and through the Son whom God sent when His people had refused to hear the voices of His servants, the prophets.

The Spirit came; and He spoke in languages which all the men of Israel assembled in Jerusalem on that day of Pentecost could understand, even those Israelites who in their long sojourn abroad had unlearned their native language. Each one of them heard "the mighty works of God" told in his own tongue. They responded with amazement, for which the sound as of a roaring wind from heaven and the sight of apportioned tongues provided grounds enough; with perplexity at the ecstatic utterances of the apostles, which broke through the quiet habits of their piety; and with that feeble mockery by which men fight their way out of a mysterious and disquieting twilight zone back into the clear daylight of common sense: "They are filled with new wine."

Still the Holy Spirit comes where and when it pleases God to send Him to proclaim the wonderful works of God. How will we respond? Will we stop short at amazement and perplexity, shaking our heads at some of His stranger (and lesser) manifestations? Will we even stoop to mockery at those manifestations of the Spirit which strike us as bizarre, so that we may ignore the rest of them and proceed to the usual order of business?

Or shall we find grace to go the way Jesus went under the impulsion of the Spirit — the way into the wilderness to meet and overcome the Tempter, the way into the Scripture and obedience to the Father's voice heard in the Scriptures, the way into self-consuming ministry and so into that life over which death has no more authority? Shall we find grace to go the way which the first church went in obedience to the Spirit? The first church did not shrink from ecstasy where ecstasy was the Spirit's gift; neither did she shrink from obedience to the Spirit's will of love. The church that spoke with tongues and felt the earth shake under her feet at the Spirit's presence went soberly about the work of providing for her poor, selling property, and electing as officials men of Spirit and wisdom to that end. The Spirit-filled church went about the work of witness and apology, of mission and martyrdom; she did not even shrink from that dangerous work which has probably killed more

Christians than persecution ever did: the sour labor of controversy.

It is the purpose of this little book to consider the power and the presence of the Holy Spirit in His temple, the church; to let men hear His voice calling on them to live the life which He, the Giver of life, can give to help men move at least one small step beyond amazement and perplexity and a long step away from mockery toward the obedience of faith. Let us dare to believe the promise and hope to inherit the promise.

Life and Liberty

The law of the Spirit of life in Christ Jesus has set me free from the law of sin and death. (Rom. 8:2)

The coming of the Holy Spirit is an event, a gift and act of God as real, as down-to-earth, and as irreversible as the coming of Christ. The coming of Christ has left its indelible mark on history; since His coming, the old order has passed and a new order prevails. Time is split up into B. C. and A. D. The old division, once set by God Himself between Jew and Gentile, has ceased to signify anything; the only question that is still meaningful is whether a man is for Christ or against Him. So the coming of the Spirit ushers in a new age, a new order of things, a new community, a new people of God. We who write "the year of our Lord Jesus Christ" could with equal fitness write "the year of the Holy Spirit, the Lord and Giver of life," for the coming of the Spirit is the full coming of our Lord Jesus Christ. The Spirit completes the presence of Christ on earth until the day of His return.

As the coming of Christ claims all men for His lordship, so the coming of the Spirit lays His gift and His claim upon man. With the coming of the Spirit into the world at Pentecost, with the coming of the Spirit into our lives at our baptism, we are confronted with a graciously imperious and controlling order of things which presses in upon us all and claims us all—all, not only a small spiritual elite but all of us garden-variety baptized men, women, and children in the whole compass of our ordinary lives.

Paul calls this order of things "the law of the Spirit." As the Law is the very Word and will of God, is God Himself, the Deliverer of His people, laying claim to His redeemed people, so the Spirit is God's presence among us, really and articulately addressing us, ordering the life of God's people, putting into force His salutary orders in the city of God and in the hearts of its citizens. The Spirit is *there*, as real and as potent as the unnoticed air we breath, as real and active as the wind which cools our broth or bellies our sails. We cannot ignore Him. For to ignore Him is to ignore God as He draws near us. If we ignore Him, we defy Him; and we know what that rebellion meant for God's people of old:

> But they rebelled
> and grieved His Holy Spirit;
> therefore He turned to be their enemy,
> and Himself fought against them. (Is. 63:10)

Why should anyone attempt to ignore Him or dare to defy Him? Ah, that is the deep mystery of the malice of Adam, who willed to be "like God" and fled from the Creator who went searching for him on the garden paths of Eden. It is the inborn malice of all the sons of Adam who inherit his fatal will and join him in his godless flight. For the "law of the Spirit" is the pure grace of "the forgiveness of sins, the resurrection of the body, and the life everlasting" which we confess in our Creed. The Spirit's gift is new life, eternal life.

The life conferred by the Spirit of life is new. It is new

by contrast with our old life under the law of sin and death. The liberation He brings confers on us more than any of the fancied freedoms that we dream about so hotly and scream for so loudly, although we half know in the midst of our dreams and screams that these freedoms will leave us still unsatisfied. The Spirit sets us free with a genuine freedom, freedom from the ancient compulsion to sin, freedom from that dreadful judgment of God which locks us up and holds us fast in our rebellion against Him, bound to do what we fatally want to do. He liberates us from that living death when each motion of our unfree will and each action of our fettered hands is guilt and punishment in one, a suicidal life-in-death. Jesus Christ broke the stranglehold which sin and death had on man when He drank the cup our sin had mixed and when He endured and triumphed over death. The "law of the Spirit of life" makes His single victory the victory of us all, the present and potent divine reality which claims the lives of all who believe in Him.

The life conferred by the Spirit of life is new also absolutely, that is, new not only by contrast with the old but by virtue of its quality as "life in Christ Jesus." "Christ being raised from the dead will never die again; death no longer has dominion over Him. The death He died He died to sin, once for all, but the life He lives He lives to God." "Life in Christ Jesus" is human life as it has not been since Adam, life to the hilt, life to be lived to the full, the feast of God with no death's head at the feast, no sword suspended over the feaster's head, no moving finger suddenly writing doom upon the wall. Life is no longer merely death deferred; this is life that breathes the fresh eternal air which rushes into the vacuum left by the destruction of death.

"In obedience to the law lies liberty," the old saw has it. In obedience to the law of the Spirit of life lies liberty unlimited and endless life.

Not Crawling but Walking

God has done what the Law, weakened by the flesh, could not do: sending His own Son in the likeness of sinful flesh and for sin, He condemned sin in the flesh, in order that the just requirement of the Law might be fulfilled in us, who walk not according to the flesh but according to the Spirit. (Rom. 8:3-4)

Omnia mea mecum porto "I carry all my possessions with me"—an ancient philosopher, proud of his philosophic self-sufficiency, once said. We would echo that statement ruefully. We do carry everything that is really ours with us—and we cannot get rid of it. We carry with us the past which none of us can bend out of its eternal shape: the long past running back to Adam with its heritage of revolt and guilt; the short past of 20, 30, 40, 50 years with its unkept promises and its ruined years; my past pocked by

> . . . that sin, through which I run,
> And do run still; though still I do deplore . . .
> . . . that sin which I did shun
> A year or two; but wallowed in a score.

We carry with us ourselves, our "flesh"; we cannot get rid of that son of Adam with Adam's rebellious blood flowing in his veins, who pays lip service to God's law but lacks the strength and the will to obey the law, so that our history under God's law is the record of "what the law could not do," the chronicle of the law's failure and our guilt.

Omnia mea mecum porto. God help me, for I cannot endure what I must bear. God has helped me; He has helped us all. He has done what the Law with its "Thou shalt" could not do. The words of the Law bounced like hailstones off our too, too solid flesh; we may have been stung by them but we were not changed by them. When the Law was impotent and we were helpless, God sent His Son "for sin," to deal with sin, into the hell which we had made. The Son made Himself one with us; He came to gasp and groan and die "in the likeness of sinful flesh," there where sin had its stranglehold on us. And there God destroyed the strangler. Where men in their desperation cursed God and died, the Son held firm in God. He cried "My God," and dying committed His spirit into the Father's hands. This one innocent Man comprehended us all in His obedient love and so broke the strangler's hold on man. When the strangler, namely, sin, was condemned, he was destroyed, for with God there is no gap between the verdict of condemnation and the execution of the verdict. The crisis that canceled the guilt of sin once for all has broken the power of sin.

God has helped us; and His help endures, not merely as a bright, inspiring memory of what happened once but as a present inspiring power. All that God did once in His Son is present and active in the liberating and enlivening power of His Spirit, in "the law of the Spirit of life in Christ Jesus." Through the Spirit God conforms us to the image of His Son, so that the Son becomes the Firstborn among many brethren, among sons on whose lips is the Son's word of devotion:

Lo, I have come to do Thy will, O God;
as it is written of Me in the roll of the book. (Heb. 10:7)

The law of God is no longer external to us whom God has conformed to the image of the Firstborn, no longer a terrifying "Thou shalt." Each of us can say, "I delight in the law of God according to my inmost self." The "just requirement of the Law" that we be the men God created us to be, men who love God and love their neighbor—the just requirement that we be in act what God has declared us to be in Christ and in fact—comes to be fulfilled in us. It is fulfilled in us because God's Spirit is living and working in us, inspiring and enabling us to "walk according to the Spirit." The Spirit's power is attested not only in the ecstatic and inarticulate cry born of the fervor of our longing hope but also in every little act of forbearance, forgiveness, and self-sacrificing affection which reflects, however feebly, the love of God in Christ. Each such act is a step in the walk according to the Spirit; each is a triumph of God's Spirit over our flesh.

While this earth stands and this age runs, our Yes to the Spirit will be an embattled No to the flesh. None of us walks according to the Spirit in an uninterrupted line of triumphal progress; we all lurch and stagger under the tug and intoxication of the flesh, and we pray, "Forgive us our trespasses," daily as the Son has taught us. But thanks be to God, we *walk*. Men who "walk according to the flesh" do not really walk; they crawl on their bellies and eat dust, possessed by an insatiable hunger for the dust that is killing them. We *walk,* and ever and again there are those exhilarating times that all devoted walkers know: those times when we walk in God's free air and walking ceases to be foot-slogging and becomes the free, swinging, automatic motion of man-as-he-ought-to-be, of free man—free to enjoy the sky, the air, the beautiful faces of his fellow travelers, the incredible loveliness of the flowers soon to fade and never to be seen again, free to go where our hearts are free to love and our tongues are free to praise. We walk as the Son once walked in Galilee, with an eye for the lilies of the field and the birds of the air and a heart for all men. "We all . . . reflecting the glory of the Lord, are being changed into His likeness from one degree of glory to another."

Omnia mea mecum porto. We need no longer carry with us all that is ours. We are privileged; we have become bearers of the Spirit and of all that is God's—His Word, His grace, the unutterable gift of His beloved Son.

The Christian's New Mind-Set

Those who live according to the flesh set their minds on the things of the flesh, but those who live according to the Spirit set their minds on the things of the Spirit. To set the mind on the flesh is death, but to set the mind on the Spirit is life and peace. For the mind that is set on the flesh is hostile to God; it does not submit to God's law, indeed it cannot; and those who are in the flesh cannot please God. But you are not in the flesh, you are in the Spirit, if in fact the Spirit of God dwells in you. Anyone who does not have the Spirit of Christ does not belong to Him. (Rom. 8:5-9)

"Now, let's be realistic about this." Anyone with experience in committee meetings and consultations has learned what this preamble suggests. It usually introduces a suggestion for a mean and grubby compromise, a proposal that we settle for something less than whole honesty and complete candor, that we decline to face all the facts, that black-and-white be converted into a tolerable shade of gray, that the forthright either-or become a both-and, that the edge be taken off a sharp situation with a neat "while we realize, of course . . . still, it must be borne in mind . . . ."

The prophets and apostles, the bearers and champions of God's Word, will not permit us to be anything but realistic; but they force us to be really realistic: to see black as black and to call it black, to acknowledge white as white and to call it white. Jeremiah, for example, has sharp words for "prophets who prophesy lies . . . who prophesy the deceit of their own heart" (Jer. 23:26-27), who think to make God's people forget His uncompromising name by feeding them on their dreams. He threatens the people who listen to them with "everlasting reproach and perpetual shame" (Jer. 23:40). When God's men say realism, they mean realism.

Paul, in the words before us, bids us be realistic about ourselves, not in order to suggest an evasion or a compromise but in order to arm us for battle and to lead us to victory. He bids us look open-eyed and unafraid at what we are, whither we are going, what the Holy Spirit is, and whither His victorious life is tending. We are to be realistic in order that we may fight God's battle and that His victory may be ours.

What are we? We are "flesh," men doomed to live and die under the "law of sin and death." But not only are we flesh because we can't avoid it; we are flesh because that is what we want to be. Being flesh is not merely our doom; it is our desire. We "set our minds" on the flesh; we are voluntarily "hostile" to God. We cannot submit to God's law, to be sure; but this failure is a failure of our willing, and it is our guilt. There is a dark mystery here which eludes the analysis of our minds but proves itself painfully true to our consciences. We *cannot* please God; and as flesh we *do not want* to please God, to render Him free and willing service.

We choose to be God's enemies; we elect to do battle with God. He who does battle with God has thereby signed his own death warrant, for "to set the mind on the flesh is death." How long we may survive to carry on this futile fight against God, is not really significant. When we join the army that fights against God, we have entered the ranks of the living dead. If "flesh" were all, the story of our days would end with a long, discordant cry on a dark stage. Some of us might be able to put some measure of defiance, some sort of tragic splendor, into the cry; but the act and the play would end as they always do: "A cry is heard, the curtain falls."

But "flesh" is not all, and the discordant cry on the dark stage need not be the end of the play. The play must and does have in it a farewell, a long farewell to all *our* greatness. That is why prophet and apostle force us to be realists, that we may see how the tragedy of flesh ends and that we may learn to look elsewhere for the possibility of another and better ending. Unless we have learned to say with Paul: "Wretched man that I am! Who will deliver me from this body of death?" we shall never learn to say: "Thanks be to God, who gives us the victory through our Lord Jesus Christ."

Jesus Christ our Lord has rewritten the story of our days; and He has given us His Spirit to enable us to play a new and better role in the story. There, in the Spirit, is a power of a kind different from and greater than the power by which we win or lose our battles:

> Not by might, nor by power,
> but by My Spirit,
> says the Lord of hosts. (Zech. 4:6)

Here is a power before which the great mountain of earthly opposition becomes a plain. Here is a power before which great world powers (such as Egypt with its splendid cavalry was in Isaiah's day) appear as the futile and fumbling things that they are:

The Egyptians are men, and not God;
   and their horses are flesh, and not spirit.
When the Lord stretches out His hand,
   the helper will stumble, and he who is helped will fall,
and they will all perish together. (Is. 31:3)

The Spirit does His work where a show of force can do nothing, where horses and chariots and all the mighty claptrap of sophisticated armaments must fail. He works in our hearts. He can give us a mind whose goal and end is not death, a mind at peace with God, no longer hostile, able to think thoughts and to will deeds that live in the sunshine of God's pleasure—thoughts and deeds whose goal and end are "life and peace."

All this is real and simple, as near and as actual as our baptism. Paul is the realist here too; he ends by speaking not of dreams and hopes but of reality: "You are not in the flesh, you are in the Spirit."

Bearing the Mark of Jesus

If the Spirit of Him who raised Jesus from the dead dwells in you, He who raised Christ Jesus from the dead will give life to your mortal bodies also through His Spirit which dwells in you. (Rom. 8:11)

We are marked men, we who have been baptized and have received the Spirit. We have upon us the imprint of Jesus, the first Man in whom God's promise found fulfillment: "I will pour out My Spirit on *all* flesh." (Joel 2:28)

Jesus was "flesh" indeed at the moment when He stood in Jordan's waters to receive the baptism of John. He was wholly "in the likeness of sinful flesh" when He overruled the Baptist's astonished objection and by submitting to John's baptism made Himself one with a people wholly under the impending wrath of God. It was there, in the flesh, that He saw the heavens opened and the Spirit of God descending upon Him. It was there that the voice from heaven hailed Him as the beloved Son upon whom God's good pleasure rests. There the flesh of man (comprehended in Jesus' manhood) learned to pray again the child's prayer of familiar love which begins with the child's confident address of "Abba!"

There the mark of Jesus began to be imprinted on us men; there we began to be marked as sons of God taught by the Spirit to cry "Abba!" And there we received the mark of the resurrection and the life of the world to come. When the heavens opened to Jesus and the Spirit descended on Him, man was being welcomed into the new world of God which Jesus was to win for man. For the Son who cries "Abba!" death cannot be the end. Jesus in His love dies the sinner's death, once for all. But He dies in the sure hope of the beloved Son. The hope which moved Jesus to conclude His every prediction of suffering and death with the words, "And on the third day be raised" — that hope will not be put to shame. He "who for the joy that was set before Him endured the cross, despising the shame," is seated in the Son's rightful place "at the right hand of the throne of God," one with Him in merciful majesty. God has made Him whom His people crucified "both Lord and Christ," the Lord before whom every knee shall bow, the Christ, the anointed King from David's line who "shall be great to the ends of the earth." He rose from the dead to be the Firstborn among many brethren, and in His love He calls us, in whom the Spirit dwells, His brethren. As surely as the mark of "the life of the world to come" was on Jesus, that mark is on us.

In the assurance of His sonship and of the joy set before Him Jesus went the way of the Servant — went in that astonishing, purposeful certitude to which all the evangelists bear witness. It was the certitude of the Servant who knew from the prophet Isaiah the promise written over His ministry of shame and death:

> Behold, My Servant shall prosper,
> He shall be exalted and lifted up,
> and shall be very high. (Is. 52:13)

If we are privileged to bear the mark of Jesus, the obedient Son, and the mark of the life of the world to come which His Spirit has inscribed upon us, we are privileged also to bear the mark of the Servant. By the power of that Spirit, through whom God has raised Jesus from the dead and will give life to our mortal bodies, these mortal bodies of ours can even now become Servant-bodies — bodies offered to God as living sacrifices. By the power of that Spirit things deemed impossible can be ours: we can aspire to Jesus' steady composure in the face of all the flickering malice that bedeviled Him and all the fumbling weakness of His followers that clogged His steps; can aspire to Jesus' spontaneous obedience to the Father's Word and will and His unclouded understanding of that Word and will; dare aspire to Jesus' freedom to love with the lavish and reckless generosity of the Father; dare aspire to His willingness to expend Himself for others—all that made His life the beginning and the pledge of the life of the world to come can be at work in us and through us. We can ride the cresting wave of God's purpose which will break upon the shore destined to be our everlasting and delightful home.

Dying in Order to Live

So then, brethren, we are debtors, not to the flesh, to live according to the flesh—for if you live according to the flesh you will die, but if by the Spirit you put to death the deeds of the body you will live. For all who are led by the Spirit of God are sons of God. (Rom. 8:12-14)

"We are debtors . . . put to death . . . led by the Spirit." Obligation, warfare, submission—this seems to be in strange and sharp contrast to the Spirit as Author of liberty and life with which Paul began. Paul seems to be inconsistent. Yet he himself does not seem to be aware of any inconsistency; rather, he feels that what he is now saying is a natural and valid consequence of what he has been saying heretofore. He introduces the new thought with, "So then." We had better learn to think apostolically, as Paul the servant of Jesus Christ thought, before we call him inconsistent.

"We are debtors." Our notion of freedom is so colored by our conception of freedom as an autonomous and arbitrary doing-as-we-please-and-who-is-there-to-stop-us? that Paul is obliged to use strong language—even language that is, strictly speaking, inappropriate—in order to describe genuine, true freedom properly. Because of the weakness of our flesh (which will always interpret freedom as "an opportunity for the flesh" to gratify its old desires), he speaks of the freedom that is ours in the Spirit as an *enslavement, an enslavement* to God. We need to be told by Spirit-enlightened men what true freedom is: that freedom in which "the love of Christ controls us." We need to be told that we are the forgiven debtor of Jesus' parable; we must be given ears to hear the voice of the forgiving Father: "I forgave you all that debt because you besought Me; and *ought* not you have had mercy on your fellow servant, as I had mercy on you?" We need the Spirit to teach us to cease fighting for the false freedom of our fevered dreams and to pray instead for true freedom:

> Make me a captive, Lord,
> And then I shall be free;
> Force me to render up my sword,
> And I shall conqueror be.
>
> I sink in life's alarms
> When by myself I stand;
> Imprison me within Thy arms,
> And strong shall be my hand.

"Led by the Spirit." We learn under the Spirit's tutelage that life under the law of the Spirit of life is not a sort of blissful trance. It is not a charismatic "high" but the full, waking, responsible life of a *man* — man as God created him to be and has always wanted him to be: His freely obedient son. We are led, yes, but not as manacled prisoners are led in lockstep toward no goal that they can hope for or desire, and not as sternly disciplined troops are led, with every individual will blocked out and replaced by the will of the one man in command. We are led as a son is led, as a child is led who puts his hand into the hand of a beloved and trusted father, controlled and directed not so much by the pressure of the hand that holds him as by the promptings of his heart. Under the leadership of the

Spirit the old tension between "I ought" and "I will" disappears; we learn to say in one breath with Paul: "I am under obligation" and "I am eager." We late-born sons learn to follow in the steps of the Firstborn, to be led like Him into freedom—the freedom to speak an unbroken yes to the Father's Word and to live by every word that proceeds from His mouth, refusing to compromise with the magic which degrades God by putting Him to the test, refusing to flaw the crystal bowl of obedience with the almost imperceptible crack of a negligible single obeisance to the Tempter.

Sons led by the Spirit, following the Son, learn soon enough that there can be no neutrality and no compromise. To be led by the Spirit is to be led into battle, as the Son was led, where we must fight if we would win. We *must,* as surely as we are led by the Spirit, "put to death the deeds of the body," the sinful body which is the expressive instrument of the disobedient Adam who lives in each of us and fights the desperate rearguard action of the defeated. The hands that pick and steal, finger the trigger, or point in scorn must die if the hands that bless and give are to live. The feet that are swift to shed blood must be brought to a dead halt if there are to be beautiful feet running upon the mountain to bring good news to men. The eyes that look askance and lust must be plucked out if there are to be eyes that are ever toward the Lord and alert to the needs of men.

"So then"—because the Spirit has set us free and has given us life—we are debtors who freely pay the immortal debt of love; we are living men who know the value of life and can find the heart to put to death anything which threatens our new life. The living breath of God has breathed upon us and has made us sons of the living God. The fresh salt air of the wind of God has carried out of that stinking sea of living death where we lay becalmed and doomed. Shall we strike sail and not let that mighty breath fill our sails and blow us shoreward to the Son's eternal home?

From Fear to Fellowship with Christ

You did not receive the spirit of slavery to fall back into fear, but you have received the spirit of sonship. When we cry, "Abba! Father!" it is the Spirit Himself bearing witness with our spirit that we are children of God, and if children, then heirs, heirs of God and fellow heirs with Christ, provided we suffer with Him in order that we may also be glorified with Him. (Rom. 8:15-17)

"This can't be it. There has to be a better way." What is meant is a better way to live and die than the one we know or any human being has ever known, something better than this biological crawl from birth to death that we call life. There may be some happy and tranquil temperaments who never know this feeling, but it comes to most of us as the years go by, either as a passing mood that curses the day of our birth or as a settled temper of disillusionment which resigns itself to welcoming fugitive beauty and pitying fugitive suffering without forgetting for one moment how fugitive they are. Most men, at bottom all men, know this feeling; and whether they deal with it by fury and rebellion or find some analgesic to render it bearable does not really matter much. The cloud hangs over the human race and will not go away, and that cloud is fear, the fear of the slave who lives under the domination of an arbitrary and cruel master.

> As flies to wanton boys, so are we to the gods;
> they kill us for their sport.

Not all men have felt it so cruelly or expressed it so brutally as that; but the fear lives in all men. Even the sunny rationality of the Greeks could not rid itself of the specter of the jealousy of the gods or convince itself that the gods are "careless gods" who neither punish nor reward. The "spirit of slavery" is a mighty spirit, not so readily dispelled. Even the church is visited by it in days like ours when we drink the bitter waters of defeat and eat the moldy bread of men's contempt.

We need to be reminded therefore: There is a better way, a better way than any sighing aspirations of man have dared to dream of, the way of the God who "is able to do far more abundantly than all that we ask or think," the God who has prepared for those who love Him

> What no eye has seen, nor ear heard,
> nor the heart of man conceived. (1 Cor. 2:9)

He has taken the old fear out of the life of man; He sent His Son into the dark shadow of our fear, there "to be greatly distressed and troubled . . . sorrowful, even to death," in an agony that made sweat pour from His face "like great drops of blood falling down upon the ground." The accumulated fear of all mankind, taken from us and laid on Him, pressed down on Him there in Gethsemane. He took our fear and through His Spirit gave us His trustful children's prayer. The cloud that hung over mankind enclosed the Son of Man and was lifted up from us, so that we might once more look unafraid upon the face of God, "who gives to all men generously and without reproachings," and cry "Abba! Father!" The Spirit, who is the Author of that prayer, through it witnesses to our spirit that we are children of God. In praying like children we are assured that we are children.

Made confident by the Spirit, we pray confidently to Him whose giving knows no limit; He gives "generously" and "without reproaching." Such is His will to give and give that we need not fear that we shall ever hear the impatient Father's reproach: "What, you here again?" And so that same act of the Spirit which takes away fear opens up to us the future, God's future, the Father's future. We sons of the Father are heirs of that generous Father, fellow inheritors with Christ. God has said it; God will do it. His testament will hold, whatever else in heaven or on earth may break. The glory of the world to come is ours.

We reflect the glory of our Lord Jesus Christ, the prime Heir. Under the creative breath of His Spirit we "are being changed into His likeness from one degree of glory to another; for this comes from the Lord who is Spirit." We walk through the world wrapped in the glory of the world to come; and that means suffering, for men robed in glory are not universally beloved. They in their glory expose the glory of the world as the shoddy tinsel-glory that it is. Their music of the world to come takes away the charm of the lean and flashy songs of those who belong to the earth-bound "musicians' union." And members of that "union" have ways of dealing with mavericks, painful and humiliating ways. But what of that? The old fear is gone, and God's future is opened. We know that "this slight momentary affliction is preparing for us an eternal weight of glory beyond all comparison." Again: "In all these things we are more than conquerors through Him who loved us." He loved us, and His love is no faded memory; it is ever-present, green and living, "poured into our hearts through the Holy Spirit which has been given to us."

The Homecoming Saint

And not only creation but we ourselves, who have the first-fruits of the Spirit, groan inwardly as we wait for adoption as sons, the redemption of our bodies. For in this hope we were saved. Now hope that is seen is not hope. For who hopes for what he sees? But if we hope for what we do not see, we wait for it with patience. Likewise the Spirit helps us in our weakness; for we do not know how to pray as we ought, but the

Spirit Himself intercedes for us with sighs too deep for words. And He who searches the hearts of men knows what is the mind of the Spirit, because the Spirit intercedes for the saints according to the will of God. (Rom. 8:23-27)

The saint—Paul calls us "saints"—is an odd person. It is not his halo or his robe that makes him odd and sets him apart from other men; indeed, the usual paraphernalia of sainthood are curiously absent from Paul's portrait of the saint. Paul's saint looks very much like any man who walked or walks the streets of Rome or New York. What is odd about the saint is that he is, to begin with, a being that has life and breath; he is, literally speaking, an animal. He is man, a part of creation, a product of God's commanding word and an artifact of His shaping hand, just as heaven and earth, lands and seas, birds and beasts are. He is tied to all creation, involved in all creation's weal or woe; it was man's will to be "like God" that plunged creation into futility and put the good earth under the curse of God.

The record of man's rebellion and of God's judgment upon it is written into the groaning creation round about him, an abiding memorial to man's revolt, a perpetual reminder of his guilt—guilt not only for the observed and recorded rape of his environment but also for his primal assault upon God's good creation. And so it is that when creation groans in longing for what once was when the world was young, and when it lives on only in the sure promise of God—yes, when creation groans—man groans also, and the saints among men groan most of all.

For the saint knows what he has lost and why he has lost it. He knows too that there is One who has raised up the fallen world and that there is a sure hope for him and for his fallen world, for the saint has the "firstfruits of the Spirit," a foretaste of the yet-to-come new and transfigured world where he shall be at home once more. He has received "the Spirit of adoption," is marked and sealed as God's son, and the Spirit already dwells in that body which has heretofore been the home and stronghold of indwelling sin. The saint hopes in the confidence inspired by the Spirit, who brings into our present life the Christ who once took on our body and became in person God's No to our sin and His Yes to His creation. He hopes for the gift of his redeemed body, a body that will be the proper instrument and expression of the Spirit that is in him.

The saint is on his way home—a homing bird. But he is no mere homing pigeon moving on wings impelled by dumb instinct. He is a willing and thinking homing man. In the Word which the Spirit speaks to him he hears the Father's invitation, "Come home!" and is assured of the Father's welcome for a lost son. He drinks the traveler's cup and eats traveler's bread in the supper which the Spirit spreads for him, a supper which is both the recall, real and living, of a past fellowship with the Lord who walked the homeward way before him and the anticipation of the joyous meal and music that await him in the Father's house.

The homing saint cannot but pray for his homecoming. But it is just here that he is most conscious of his weakness: he cannot pray for his homecoming as he ought. The far-off home is so different from anything the traveler has as yet known. The hold of traveler's habits is so strong, the weariness of travel so oppressive, and the traveler's horizon so narrow that he cannot find the heart or the words to pray with the eloquence and the insistence that befits the prayer. "They kingdom come" becomes rote and routine. But it is also just here, in the faltering of his prayer, that he experiences the aid of the Spirit: "The Spirit helps us *in our weakness*," not by increasing our knowledge and making us celestial wiseacres who frame more elaborate and artistic prayers, but by strengthening our will to make better travelers of us, unwearied and persevering goers-home. "The Spirit intercedes for us with sighs too deep for words," sighs that catch the ear of God because they are prayers according to His will. His will is that all His sons come home to Him, to find in Him the paradise which they have lost.

Aglow with the Spirit

Never flag in zeal, be aglow with the Spirit, serve the Lord.
(Rom. 12:11)

"Be aglow"—that reminds us of the people we see in advertisements, those radiant, effervescent people enraptured over their new cars, seat covers, appliances, hair-driers, after-shave lotions, soft drinks, a whiskey more expensive than they have been able to afford before, or pillows and mattresses (this happy breed of men even sleep radiantly, however they may manage that). We know, of course, that these wonderfully dynamic and exuberant people exist only in the imagination of the gentlemen from Madison Avenue who created them. But we know too that the men from Madison Avenue have a keen sense for whatever hidden impulses move mankind, and they are quick to exploit man's deep, inarticulate desires. They know that we are all dissatisfied with our gray, muted lives of low expectations and small satisfactions, that we want to be "aglow" with something even if we do not know and cannot imagine clearly what we want to be "aglow" with.

Paul offers us the radiant life in pithy, nonluxuriant language, as if it were there for the asking and to be had for the taking. And it is for he says: "If you confess with your lips that Jesus is Lord and believe in your heart that God raised Him from the dead, you will be saved"—in other words, the radiant life, the new life seething with an unearthly vitality, is yours.

To confess Jesus as Lord is to have Him as your Lord. To believe in your heart that God has raised Him from the dead is to believe that "Christ died and rose again that He might be Lord of the dead and of the living," Lord in the power of His Spirit, who brings His lordship into our lives and maintains our loyalty to His lordship. To be aglow with the Spirit is to live under the bright and lively lordship of Him who is the Light of the world.

That is why the almost casual command, "Be aglow with the Spirit," is bracketed by "never flag in zeal," on the one hand, and by "serve the Lord," on the other. Being "turned on" by the Spirit is no vague mood and no mystic trance; it is a conscious, personal relationship to Him in whose face we have seen the reasons for which we would fain call Him Master. It means that we said to our Lord, "I will follow You wherever You go." We have set our hand to the plow and will not cast a lingering, longing look backward; we will not flag in zeal when our zeal if tested and tried. Being aglow with the Spirit means that we have heeded Jesus' call of "Come unto Me" and have in Him found rest for our souls; that His easy yoke rests on our willing shoulders and gives guidance to our fumbling lives; that our distraught and distracting desires have been overruled by the one desire to serve the Lord.

Is such a life the prerogative of a few favored souls or is it possible also for plain, garden-variety Christians like us? Our Lord intended it for us all; He prayed the Father and gave the Spirit that we might all have His joy fulfilled in us. As for Paul, there is nothing to indicate that he was by native disposition an optimistic and ebulliently cheerful man, prone to expect more of the ordinary man than the ordinary man can give. The strain of transfigured joy which runs through his Letter to the Philippians (written from jail) must be set down to the account of the Holy Spirit. The Christians of Philippi, of whom he confidently expected a joy which should echo his own, were a lovable lot, to be sure; but they were no gold-plated saints, and their halos went askew. The weeds of "grumbling and questioning" grew in their garden; and at least two of their ladies marred an admirable previous record by getting into each other's hair in an unsaintly way. And all down the years the church, "by schisms rent asunder, by heresies distressed," has left monuments to the flaming presence of the Spirit in her creeds, her songs, her music, her architecture, her sculpture and painting, her stained glass that turns daylight into doxologies, and in all her simple, unrecorded arts of selfless love which we know happened then because they are happening now to us and among us who hear the same Word and are set aglow by the same Spirit.

Abounding in Hope

Welcome one another, therefore, as Christ has welcomed you, for the glory of God. For I tell you that Christ became a servant to the circumcised to show God's truthfulness in order to confirm the promises given to the patriarchs and in order that the Gentiles might glorify God for His mercy. . . . May the God of hope fill you with all joy and peace in believing, so that by the power of the Holy Spirit you may abound in hope (Rom. 15:7-9, 13)

The church at Rome was a normal church. It was made up of men and women who had been baptized and had received the Holy Spirit. There men and women were, as Paul generously acknowledged, "full of goodness, filled with all knowledge, and able to instruct one another." They were "God's beloved in Rome, called to be saints." They were also walking demonstrations of the man described by Paul in chapter seven as both saint and sinner, not above "disputes over opinions," prone to "despise" and "pass judgment on" one another. The occasion of these disputes and the contemptuous and carping behavior to which they gave rise was a trifling matter; in the long perspective of the years in which we see it, it seems downright silly. But anything that threatens to disrupt the fellowship of the church for which Christ died and rose is not a trifling matter, and to men trapped in colliding convictions and abrasive association the matter did not seem silly, and they would be ill served by an apostle who would call it silly.

Paul serves the beloved saints in Rome better than that. He invokes upon them the blessing of "the God of hope," to the end that they may be filled "with all joy and peace in believing" and "the power of the Holy Spirit." And all this to the end that they "may abound in hope." The Holy Spirit has the power to make vividly present what is long past and to move the distant future into the realm of our present experience.

When we confess our faith in the Holy Spirit we must speak not only of the present ("one holy Christian and apostolic church") but also of the long-gone past ("who spoke by the prophets") and the far-off future ("the resurrection of the dead and the life of the world to come"). The power of the Holy Spirit makes us contemporary with the patriarch Abraham, the homeless, landless, childless nomad to whom God promised His blessing, who believed the promise in hope against hope. The power of the Spirit makes us contemporary with the people descended from Abraham, the people to whom God gave a future and a hope when all possibilities of hoping seemed ended. When the whole house of Israel said, "Our bones are dried up and our hope is lost; we are clean cut off," Israel's prophet sees (and lets us see) the dry bones in the valley reclothed with flesh and sinews, living and standing upon their feet, a great host. The power of the Spirit makes us contemporary with Christ and His faithful ministry to the Jew, that no word of God's promises might fall to the ground unconfirmed and unfulfilled. The power of the Spirit makes us contemporary with the last Gentile to join the motley ranks of those who "glorify God for His mercy," that "great multitude . . . standing before the throne and before the Lamb, clothed in white robes, with palm branches in their hands, and crying with a loud voice, 'Salvation belongs to our God who sits upon the throne, and to the Lamb.'"

Thus the God of hope fills us with exultant and thankful joy and gives us happiness and health "in believing" as we become contemporary with all His past mighty acts. Thus He makes us "abound in hope" as the Spirit makes us contemporary with those future acts of His which shall say Amen to all His promises. We learn to *"abound* in hope"; we become high-hearted and large-hearted men, capable of something more than the democratic virtue of toleration—good and to-be-prized as that rare plant in the gardens of mankind is. We become capable of *welcoming* men of all sorts: men of the wrong color whom we have injured, men who have injured us, men with irritating convictions stubbornly held, prejudiced men, men whose sniveling timidity casts a shadow on our bright courage. We become capable of welcoming them as Christ has welcomed us and as we surely hope He will welcome us on the Last Day: "Come, O blessed of My Father."

Ransomed Bodies

Do you not know that your body is a temple of the Holy Spirit within you, which you have from God? You are not your own; you were bought with a price. So glorify God in your body. (1 Cor. 6:19-20)

"One there is who is good," Jesus says; and it is the hallmark of His words that they everywhere presuppose that God is the Author and Initiator of all that is good. When Jesus teaches His disciples He speaks first of the God who enriches the poor, comforts all mourners, gives the earth to the meek and His righteousness to those that hunger and thirst for it—this before even mentioning any activity of the disciple. And when He comes to speak of the disciple's activity He speaks first of God's activity, of the divine love that has made them to be the salt of the earth, the light of the world, and the city set on a hill for all men to see. Then, and not until then, He bids His disciples act. How? "Let your light . . . shine before men"—as the light of lamps which God has lighted, lamps which therefore must shine to His glory—"that men may see your good words and give glory to your Father who is in heaven."

The Holy Spirit impressed this axiom of Jesus deeply on the minds of His disciples. Men as different from each other in their temperaments and in the accents of their proclamation as James and Paul are at one in the way in which they operate with this axiom. James first proclaims the God "who gives to all men generously and without reproaching," "the Father of lights," the Author of "every perfect gift," whose giving is more certain than the sure movements of the sun and moon and stars which He has created. He speaks of God's supreme gift of new life for man, bestowed by His Word of truth. Not until James has spoken thus of God's Word as His creative Word and as His saving Word does he speak of it as a Word to be done, as the perfect Law of liberty.

Paul also begins with the indisputable ("Do you not know?"), axiomatic giving goodness of God. God, he says, in His goodness and mercy has chosen the body of man, once doomed to sin and death, to be the temple of His Spirit, the place where His honor dwells in life-giving and sanctifying presence. The body, that old haunt of sin and death, was cleared and cleansed and made a quiet temple fit for the presence of the Spirit by an act of God's goodness, by the dying of God's Son, "who gave Himself for our sin to deliver us from the present evil age, according to the will of our God and Father."

We were "bought with a price," with the costly ransom of a life given for our forfeited lives. "You are not your own"; thank God for that. We need not be our own. No longer need we do what we think we want to do; no longer need we be the victims of our unleashed sensuality; no longer need we be dominated and degraded by our perverted instincts; no longer need we be turned upon one another by that base mind which makes us one another's hell. *"So"*—that is the inescapable logic of those good acts of the good God who has made us His own and has given

His Spirit to dwell in us, the logic of grace bestowed and power given: "*So* glorify God in your body." "Body" means activity. Whoever has acquired a slave's body is entitled to the slave's services. The Creator who made our body and put His blessing upon it, and the Redeemer who ransomed our body and put the mark of resurrection on it, He sets such store by our body that He claims it as the living sacrifice due to Himself and wants our activities to be a bodily worship that glorifies Him.

Only people who presume to be more spiritual than the Spirit can depreciate and despise the body. The rest of us will prize our bodies and use them to glorify God. We will so walk and work on earth that our actions will be mobile witnesses to the goodness of our good God. This need not be a bravura performance, though the Director may call for a bravura performance—like courageous dying at His discretion. The Holy Spirit can make good music to the glory of God in all manner of modes, tempos, and measures, and He knows best whether the quiet melody of a life whose beauty makes all others ugly may not be the best music to be heard by passersby when they come near His temple.

The Spirit's Greatest Gift

Now concerning spiritual gifts, brethren, I do not want you to be uninformed. You know that when you were heathen, you were led astray to dumb idols, however you may have been moved. Therefore I want you to understand that no one speaking by the Spirit of God ever says, "Jesus be cursed!" And no one can say, "Jesus is Lord" except by the Holy Spirit. (1 Cor. 12:1-3)

The Corinthian Christians were puzzled and disturbed, as many Christians are today, by some manifestations of the

Spirit's working in their church, particularly by the gift of "speaking with tongues," that gift of enraptured inarticulate speech so highly prized by some of them. Paul therefore begins his discussion of spiritual gifts by pointing to that prime and supreme gift of the Spirit which we have learned to give thanks for in the words of Luther's Small Catechism: "I believe that I cannot by my own reason or strength believe in Jesus Christ, *my Lord,* or come to Him; but the Holy Ghost has called me by the Gospel." The first and basic gift of the Spirit is that He enables us to call Jesus Lord and so put our lives under His dominion. It was the Holy Spirit, Paul reminds these new Christians, who had led them out of the murky world of paganism where they were moved by the dark and wayward impulses that govern men gone astray from God to give their loyalty and address their prayers to dumb idols. The latter could not enlighten them, as the Holy Spirit enlightens men with His gifts, and they did not answer their prayers.

Early in the history of their church the Corinthians had heard voices which attempted to drown out the cry of "Jesus is Lord." When Paul spoke to the men of the Corinthian synagog of the lordship of Jesus, "they opposed and reviled him." They were of one mind with their kinsmen by race who had cried out to Pilate, "Crucify him!" and had met the protestation of the Roman governor that Roman law found no crime in Him with an appeal to their own law, the law of Moses: *"We* have a law, and by that law he ought to die." And they browbeat Pilate into executing Him under that law. Did not Jesus hang upon the tree? Did not their law say: "A hanged man is accursed by God"? The blind logic of the law therefore led them to assert that Jesus was accursed.

The Spirit had led them out of the sultry gloom of their pagan past. He led them past the region lit with terrible clarity by the livid light of legalism, into the clear sunlight and clean air of the rainwashed morning world of which David had sung when the Spirit spoke by him of the Messiah destined to rise from David's house:

> He dawns on them like morning light,
>> like the sun shining forth upon a cloudless morning,
>> like rain that makes grass to sprout from the earth.
>>> (2 Sam. 23:4)

This is the prime and supreme gift of the Spirit: He brings us to Jesus. The validity and value of every spiritual gift are to be measured by this gift. If we are dubious about some spiritual gift, if we doubt whether it is indeed a gift of the Spirit, the question we are to ask is not, "Is it familiar, or is it strange?"; not, "Is it normal and ordinary, or does it seem bizarre?"; not, "Is it found in the mainstream traditions of the church or only among what we loftily call splinter groups?"; not, "Is it a 'manageable' gift, or is it likely to prove 'unmanageable'?" The question is: "Is this a gift of Him who led us to call Jesus Lord? Is this a gift we can lay at the feet or put into the hands of the Crucified and say, 'We give Thee but Thine own'?"

The above is the criterion which Paul employs. Are there variety and diversity in the gifts of the Spirit? The Lord Jesus shows no marked predilection for uniformity, no more than His Father in heaven, the Creator, has. In the days of His flesh He drew to Himself a colorful variety of men. His apostles included an ex-publican, an ex-Pharisee, and an ex-Zealot, and He sent them out on a variety of missions—to Jews, to Samaritans, and to Gentiles. He uttered no legislation that would cast all His followers in one mold, and He prescribed no rites that would clothe them all in identical robes of piety. What He willed and what the Spirit wills is that the prodigal variety of spiritual gifts be used "for the common good."

"When Jesus knew that His hour had come to depart out of this world to the Father, having loved His own, He loved them to the end"—that is the evangelist John's summary of the life of Jesus: love. Therefore Paul sees in love the "more excellent way," the indispensable basis and motivation for the use of every spiritual gift, that self-giving love which shall endure long after all other gifts have lost their purpose and have ceased to be.

"I will build My church," Jesus said. Therefore His apostle sets the higher value on those spiritual gifts that do most to edify, to build the church of Christ. The man who uses the Spirit's power to "edify himself" rather than the church is dangerously close to being the man who exalts himself, and the shadow of Jesus' judgment on self-exaltation has fallen on him, great charismatic though he be.

No flame of the Spirit is to be quenched; every flame is to be treasured and tended, "but all things should be done decently and in order." Those who call Jesus Lord can go only His way, the way of the One who has been called the one wholly natural, unposed Man who ever lived. Self-assertion and display dare not mar the conduct of those who follow in the footsteps of Him who called Himself "gentle and lowly in heart," the footsteps of that quiet Man who bade His zealous disciples sheathe his sword, the footsteps of that selfless Man who never used the power that was His except for others — to mend their broken lives. It is His Spirit that we have received. Shall we grieve that Spirit by attempting to be something that He could never be?

Gifts for the Service of All

To each is given the manifestation of the Spirit for the common good. (1 Cor. 12:7)

The Spirit is always given "for the common good," for a ministry to others — not for private religious self-fulfilment or for the secret raptures of the recluse. In the Old Testament the power and blessing of the Spirit was manifested in men on whom the welfare of God's people depended: in strong deliverers like Gideon and Jephthah, in anointed kings like Saul and David, in prophets like Micah and Ezekiel. And when He came who was the ultimate Deliverer, the Son of David, the Messiah on whom the Spirit rests, and the Prophet to whom all prophecy had pointed, He declared His mission in words from Isaiah which clearly marked Him as Bearer of the Spirit "for the common good":

> The Spirit of the Lord is upon Me,
>> because He has anointed Me to preach good
>> news to the poor.
> He has sent Me to proclaim release to the captives
>> and recovery of sight to the blind,
>> to set at liberty those who are oppressed.
>
>> (Luke 4:18)

Peter proclaimed Him to Cornelius and his kinsmen and friends thus: "God anointed Jesus of Nazareth with the Holy Spirit and with power . . . He went about doing good and healing all that were oppressed by the devil."

The Spirit of the Servant was promised through Isaiah:

> Behold My Servant, whom I uphold,
>> My Chosen, in whom My soul delights;
> I have put My Spirit upon Him,
>> He will bring forth justice to the nations. (Is. 42:1)

That Spirit was poured out on the apostles at Pentecost and was through their ministry given to the church, enabling men to witness to the Servant in word and deed, to serve and suffer and die "for the common good." Because "the common good" is paramount, Paul can liken the Spirit-filled church to a human body in which all "the members have the same care for one another," so that "if one member suffers, all suffer together; if one member is honored, all rejoice together." For the same reason Paul can declare that no gift has any value if there is not the love which puts each gift into the service of all, and he urges the Christians of Corinth: "Make love your aim." Therefore Paul places the higher value on those gifts that edify the whole church and has so little patience with religious virtuosos who think God's music is a series of solos written for them. "Let all things be done for edification," he says of the worship assemblies of the church, since worship is to be a reflection and summary of the whole life of the church. For of the church he says: "The whole body, joined and knit together by every joint with which it is supplied, when each part is working properly, makes bodily growth and upbuilds itself in love."

It all sounds so simple and straightforward when Paul speaks of it. The situation was simpler then, it seems, and the action called for by the situation more readily possible than now. How are we to serve the common good with the gifts of the Spirit today — we lonely men lost in crowds of isolated, solitary men, leading a meaningless existence in a system which regiments and mechanizes our lives? How are we to become operatives of the Spirit for the common good in a system that knows only a caricature of the common good and has no room for the Spirit? Even the church seems incapable of functioning rightly — spiritually — in this atmosphere. Organization and administration (Paul counts "helpers" and "administrators" among the spiritual gifts given to the church) often seem to thwart rather than further the purpose for which they were given, namely, that all members of the body function individually and purposefully for the health and well-being of the whole body. Within the church, as outside it, men remain, it seems, locked up in themselves, encrusted in their egos, existing for themselves rather than living for others.

Before we cry too pitifully into our beer (in our day self-pity is bidding for a place among the Seven Deadly Sins) we might recall that never in the history of man has the question of the common good pressed so closely and so insistently upon us as today. The ease and rapidity of worldwide communication have confronted us with the massed misery of mankind as never before. The growth and spread of worldwide organizations of mercy have given us opportunities of responding to the needs of men on a scale unknown heretofore. The "good news to the poor" can speed and triumph, can be multiplied and transmitted, by vaster human and technical means than ever before.

Above all, are not we whimpering solitaries forgetting, unconscionably, that our Lord is King of kings and Lord of lords? His state is kingly, and "they also serve who only stand and wait." I once heard a prison chaplain tell how he was so discouraged by the lack of response to his ministry, not only on the part of the prisoners but also on the part of the prison administration and its personnel, that he was ready, one Easter Monday, to resign. He went sailing to think it over in the solitude of the sea. Then it came to him: "Every day that I stay on that job is a victory. I win by just staying there." We win by just staying there where the Lord has put us: in the ranks of the uncompromised who have not bowed the knee to whatever Baal is current and popular. He will integrate each one of us and our little manifestation of the Spirit's working into the whole of the common good which He desires and designs. We may proceed always in the assurance that every act of love prompted by the Spirit makes the world richer, and we must act in the fear that every prompting of the Spirit left unheeded leaves us all the poorer.

Who can calculate or predict what any one act prompted by the Spirit will contribute to the common good? If Paul had paused to calculate the chances of contributing to the common good by writing his First Letter to the Corinthians, he would hardly have set pen to paper at all. What was the use? Life in Ephesus (where he wrote) was life on the razor's edge, not conducive to writing inspired epistles. Life in the church at Corinth was a mess and getting messier. What use to write to *them?* Yet if Paul had not written, if he had not obeyed the prompting of the Spirit for the common good, how much poorer we all should be, all we who "in every place call on the name of the Lord Jesus Christ." He wrote, amid tears sometimes, but he wrote, and wrote again when the common good was more elusive and harder to envision than it is for us today.

Wisdom and Knowledge: Choice Gifts

To one is given through the Spirit the utterance of wisdom, and to another the utterance of knowledge according to the same Spirit. (1 Cor. 12:8)

"When the best is corrupted, it becomes the worst." Paul had seen the old saw *(corruptio optimi pessima est)* proved true once more at Corinth. He had seen wisdom and knowledge corrupted, and he had come to know at first hand what harm corrupted human wisdom can do to the Gospel, and what mischief corrupted knowledge can create in the church. He had a sick bellyful of the strutting wisdom which empties the cross of Christ of its power; and he had often enough been sick at heart over the blithe and arrogant superior "knowledge" of those who rode roughshod over other men's scruples and by flaunting their "knowledge" destroyed the weak brother for whom Christ died. It would have been quite understandable and readily pardonable if he had reacted to the opposite extreme and sung the praises of a *sancta simplicitas,* as other men have done in their impatience with the vagaries of man's agile intellect.

But Paul, called by the will of God to be the apostle of Jesus Christ, did no such thing. He knew that there is a wisdom "which cannot be gotten for gold, and silver cannot be weighed as its price" (Job 28:15), a wisdom which God has bestowed on man in Christ "whom God made our wisdom." Paul knew of a "knowledge" which belongs to those who love God and which is the most precious possession a man can have: a being-known by God, a being-chosen and being-made God's own. And so Paul cannot react to the extreme. He can and will use all the power given him by God to "destroy arguments and every proud obstacle to the knowledge of God," and he can and will serve Him alone who has declared:

> I will destroy the wisdom of the wise,
> and the cleverness of the clever I will thwart.
> (1 Cor. 1:19)

But he does not react to an extreme; he reacts to the Gospel center, here as always. He treasures the Spirit's gift of "the utterance of wisdom," the words of men to whom it has been peculiarly given to see God and His purposes steadily and to see them whole. He values the Spirit's gift of "the utterance of knowledge," the words of men enabled by the Spirit to look deeply into and to grasp fully the mysteries of God.

Paul knows what so many of us in the church have so often forgotten: God created brains, and He likes them; God made the intellect, and He wants to use it. God wants to brainwash us, not in the usual sense of depriving us of any spontaneous intellectual activity of our own, but in order that we may think, conceive, imagine, question, probe, infer, conclude, be persuaded, and persuade as His free sons. To that end He gives us His Spirit. The men of the Old Testament and New Testament who "moved by the Holy Spirit spoke from God" are splendidly free and active minds—living proof that God has no preference for robots and no predilection for dullards. Whether we look at the massive architecture of the great historical works of the Old Testament that spell out in narrative the working of God's purpose for His people Israel as Israel's history moves toward its fulfilment in Christ, or at the cunningly-wrought poetry of the prophets and the Psalter, or at the strung and polished beads of wisdom in Proverbs, or at the thought-through, taut, and eloquent composition of the gospels, or at the compressed and luminous language of the epistles, or at the balanced intricacies of the Revelation to John—wherever we look we are confronted by an amount of intellectual exertion and a kind of sheer intellectual excellence that is staggering to behold.

God has uses for the diamond wit of the wise and for the magical words that poets have dreamed. Our intellect, no less than our heart and will, still feels and responds to the gravitational pull of the flesh that is God's enemy. While this world stands and these bodies live, we shall have to continue to struggle to "take every thought captive to obey Christ"; the flesh will not down, and the Spirit will not cease from mental fight. Struggling is an unpleasant, sweaty business, and we are tempted to give it up. But there is really no alternative to struggling. To say no to the mind that God created, no to the intellectual gifts of the Spirit, no to the possibilities of ministry the intellect provides and love demands — who dares speak that no?

Men Alive

Our sufficiency is from God, who has qulaified us to be ministers of a new covenant, not in a written code but in the Spirit; for the written code kills, but the Spirit gives life. (2 Cor. 3:5-6)

"Where do they come from?" the Beatles used to sing concerning "all the lonely people." Perhaps we who have been reared in the snug and lovely familiarities of the settled church have never stopped to ask that question concerning the ministers of the Gospel who preach to us and watch over us, baptizing our children, instructing our young, blessing our marriages, comforting us in our illness and bereavement, burying our dead. Perhaps we are troubled a bit when we hear that fewer and fewer young men are turning up as candidates for the ministry and that more and more ministers of the Gospel are resigning from the ministry — though the wonder of it is that any young man has ever presented himself as a candidate for the ministry and that all ministers of the Gospel have not resigned long ago. Where do they come from, this army of God's gray mice nibbling away so busily at the great mountain of the world in the forlorn hope that one day they shall have tunneled through the mountain and shall see a great light streaming through from the Other Side? Who has given these men, men with whom the church is perpetually dissatisfied (the courses of theological study are continually being revised, and new plans for in-service ministerial training burgeon annually), men never satisfied with themselves — who has given them the "sufficiency" for a task that can hardly be considered rewarding in any of the accepted senses of the term?

"Our sufficiency is from God," Paul says. God has qualified men for ministry, the ministry "of a new covenant" for He has established the new covenant. He has kept the promise which He made to His people through His servant Jeremiah in that darkest of Israel's dark hours when the Lord had dealt His people "the blow of an enemy, the punishment of a merciless foe," because His people's guilt was so great and her sin so flagrant; in that hour when Rachel, mother of the race, wept inconsolably for her children gone into captivity as a people without a future and without hope. In that hour He had promised to make a new covenant with His people, better and other than the old covenant which His ingrate people had broken — a new covenant which uttered God's enduring covenant will of "I will be your God" in terms of the forgiveness which alone could rescue the people from destruction: "I will forgive their iniquity, and I will remember their sin no more." God's forgiving grace dealt with man's sin in serious judicial majesty; He laid upon His Servant the iniquity of all. Jesus inaugurated the new covenant by making Himself an offering for sin, for on the night when He was betrayed He gave His disciples the cup with the words: "This cup is the new covenant in My blood."

With these words Jesus went into the death that was the ransom and release for all. He has released us from our ruined past, from the standing indictment of the "written code" of God's law which condemns and kills us all. He has set us free from ourselves, free from the compulsion to justify ourselves, free to accept God's justification of the ungodly for ourselves, free to receive the Spirit who puts God's law within us and writes it upon our hearts, as Jeremiah had promised. The Spirit who moves us to call God "Abba! Father!" can make our response to His will a son's glad "I can! I will!" This was something the old "written code" could not do. The best the Law could do was to wring from us a grim "I must." Now we are free to seek God and live.

Man alive—that is what God's new covenant in force, God's Spirit at work, means. Man is alive to speak God's Word and to do God's will. Because they were men alive, Peter and John replied, "We cannot but speak" when they were charged by the rulers of their people "not to speak or teach at all in the name of Jesus." And that is why there has always been and always will be an unbroken succession of men to maintain that rhythm of hearing and telling which is the beating heart of the history of the church in the world.

That is why God's gray mice keep nibbling at the beetling mountain. They have heard a word spoken by the Spirit, and they know with a certainty which no word of man can give that the great mountain is not so durable by half as it appears to be.

> What are you, O great mountain? . . . .
> You shall become a plain.

Reflectors of God's Glory

And we all with unveiled face beholding [reflecting] the glory of the Lord, are being changed into His likeness from one degree of glory to another; for this comes from the Lord who is the Spirit. (2 Cor. 3:17-18)

> Hark, the church proclaims her honor,
> And her strength is only this:
> God has laid His choice upon her,
> And the work she does is His.

Paul has been speaking of glory—of the fading glory of Moses' ministry of the Law and of the enduring glory of his own apostolic Gospel ministry of the Spirit. Distinct and disparate as these two ministries are, as disparate as life and death, they nevertheless have this in common: There is a divine glory attached to both of them, and this glory becomes a man's glory as he *acts* in obedience to God in the ministry entrusted to him. Glory is therefore not the peculiar possession of the apostle; "we *all*," all whom the Spirit has called by the Gospel and enlightened with His gifts, participate in it. For we all "reflect" the glory of the Lord who loved us and gave Himself for us.

In our words and deeds there are seen, as in a mirror, the speaking and acting love of our Lord Jesus Christ, His compassion, His will to live and die for others, in short, the glory of His grace. Where the "utterance of wisdom" is given by the Spirit, these men may see reflected Him who is in person the wisdom from above—"pure, peaceable, gentle, open to reason, full of mercy and good fruits, without uncertainty or insincerity"; where there is "the utterance of knowledge according to the same Spirit" men may hear echoed the voice of Him who said, "No one knows the Father except the Son and anyone to whom the Son chooses to reveal Him"—the voice of Him whose invitation was as wide and inclusive as His claim was high and exclusive: "Come to Me, all who labor and are heavy laden, and I will give you rest." Where faith that moves mountains is given by the same Spirit, there is the reflection of Him who, living, was determined to live by every word that proceeds from the mouth of God and, dying, committed His spirit into His Father's hands. Where the Spirit gives "gifts of healing" or "the working of miracles," there falls across man's path the luminous shadow of Him who, anointed with the Holy Spirit and with power, "went about doing good and healing all that were oppressed by the devil." Where the gift of prophecy is given, there man may hear again the Prophet mighty in word and deed for whom the disciples of Emmaus mistakenly mourned.

When the Spirit gives the gift of speaking "in various kinds of tongues," this inarticulate, ecstatic utterance is evidence that Jesus is no absent Lord; He is present and acting who trusted His Father to bring perfect praise out of the mouth of babes and to make the stones cry out if His disciples should fall silent. Where the Spirit brings forth in men the love which "bears all things, hopes all things, endures all things," these men are reflecting the glory of the Lord, "for this comes from the Lord" who is present and active in the presence and the activity of the Spirit. We whom the Spirit blesses with His gifts are the mirror of the Lord, the bright surface on which the grace of His lordship is reflected.

But we are more than mirrors, more than inert surfaces which merely reflect the Light that falls upon them. We are living men, alive by the Breath of God, and so are influenced by what we reflect as no mirror can be. We are constantly "being changed" into the likeness of our Lord; and such is the greatness of the Spirit's bounty, such the exuberance of His beneficent vitality, and such the limitless range of His creative power that this "being changed into His likeness" cannot ever come to rest. We move "from one degree of glory to another" in faith and love as we move in hope ever closer to the final glory, toward that day when He whose glory we reflect "will change our lowly body to be like His glorious body, by the power which enables Him to subject all things to Himself."

"To him who has will more be given." Whatever gift of the Spirit is ours, if it is *used* to reflect the glory of the Lord, that gift will grow, and the glory of the Lord will break more brightly upon the faces of men sitting in the valley and the shadow of death. If we "have" a gift in such a way that we do not actively have and use it, the glory of the Lord will not be darkened; God will light other candles in a million places. But if we quench the Spirit, we shall be left in darkness.

Avoiding What Is Fleshly and Foolish

Are you so foolish? Having begun with the Spirit, are you now ending with the flesh? (Gal. 3:3)

We Christians are all a bit like the man from the city who gave up his fresh-air holiday in the mountains and returned home complaining, "I'm going back to town when I can breathe properly; this air's got no body to it." The clean air of the high altitudes of the Spirit is too clean and clear for us; we long for some of the pollution that has been killing us.

So it was in the churches of Galatia in the first century. When Paul came to them with the good news of "Jesus Christ publicly portrayed as crucified" for their salvation and they heard and believed, they were baptized and received the Spirit. The Breath of God breathed on them, and they were free men breathing free clean air, no longer "in bondage to beings that by nature are no gods" but sons of a free mother born free, "sons of God through faith." Those were exhilarating days; Paul speaks of them in his Letter to the Galatians, recalling how he had first preached to the Galatians because of a bodily ailment which grounded him in Galatia, how they had made nothing of his physical condition which was a "trial" to them and might even have given rise to a superstitious aversion to the apostle. They had received him "as an angel of God, as Christ Jesus" Himself. The man whose inspired word had taught them to confess Jesus as Lord was as dear to them as their Lord, and they were ready to pluck out their eyes and give them to the man who bore on his body "the marks of Jesus."

Those exhilarating days had passed, and the Galatians soon found other voices more persuasive than Paul's, the voices of men who came with what they termed a supplement to Paul's Gospel of freedom. These voices were luring them back to the Law, back into bondage, back to the "flesh" of circumcision and the observance of days and seasons prescribed by the Law, back to the "flesh" of physical descent from Abraham, the "flesh" of man contributing something to his own salvation by his own reason or strength. When they believed and were baptized, they had "begun with the Spirit," with God's work in free and sovereign grace for their salvation; they could then say with Paul: "Through the Spirit, by faith, we wait for the hope of righteousness." Now they hoped to carry that work of God to completion with their own devisings and exertions, "with the flesh."

"O foolish Galatians!" We join Paul in that exclamation of hurt wonder. But have we 20th-century pots the right to call those first-century kettles black? We are hardly tempted in these days to revert to circumcision and the Law of Moses. And the lot of the Jew being what it is in Christian lands, who is still tempted to claim descent from Abraham? But the "flesh" is still a potent counterattraction to the Spirit; we who have begun with the Spirit in Baptism are still mightily inclined to end with the "flesh," to supplement and supplant the incredibly good Good News of what God has done by grace with a "gospel" that gives room and scope to the bright ideas and strenuosities of man, to our ingenious and squirming flesh.

We are all cater-cousins to the foolish Galatians when we decide to put "some life" into the church which is not the life of the Holy Spirit, the Lord and Giver of life; when we attempt to make the church our going concern rather than His living concern; when we think to find in our eloquence and our persuasive devices a reasonable substitute for that divine calling voice which Jesus compared with the call of the mother bird coaxing her young under her wing; when we persuade ourselves that our new and improved mind-benders will do what Christ's coaxing call alone can do. We are leaning fleshward when we feel entitled to make people promises which Jesus and His messengers never made — like promises of automatic "peace of mind" or that grandly ambiguous thing called happiness. And has not the church ceased to be the invincible bulwark against death created by the Spirit, and has it not come vulnerable "flesh," when it takes up the sword (which God gave to Caesar, not to the church) and dreams of winning victories for Christ with new-style, respectable crusades as the church that dares to kill but is afraid to die?

The Fruits of the Spirit

Walk by the Spirit, and do not gratify the desires of the flesh. For the desires of the flesh are against the desires of the Spirit, and the desires of the Spirit are against the flesh; for these are opposed to each other, to prevent you from doing what you would. But if you are led by the Spirit, you are not under the Law. Now the works of the flesh are plain: fornication, impurity, licentiousness, idolatry, sorcery, enmity, strife, jealousy, anger, selfishness, dissension, party spirit, envy, drunkenness, carousing, and the like. I warn you, as I warned you before, that those who do such things shall not inherit the kingdom of God. But the fruit of the Spirit is love, joy, peace, patience, kindness, goodness, faithfulness, gentleness, self-control; against such there is no law. And those who belong to Christ Jesus have crucified the flesh with its passions and desires. (Gal. 5:16-24)

The "desires of the flesh" and "the works of the flesh," the desires and works of man as he is — of the sons of Adam apart from God and in flight from God—these are the stuff that our news is made of. The newspapers are full of them; we are treated each day to another installment of the dreary chronicle of men's undeclared war against God.

We read each morning the chronicle of man's erotic self-assertion, which declares, "My pleasure is my god," and documents that devotion to self and defiance of God in works of "fornication, impurity, licentiousness" which even men of secular decency find distasteful and alarming.

Each morning brings a fresh chapter of man's religious self-assertion, which declares, "I'll make my own gods in my own shop and to my liking," and documents this devotion to self and defiance of the one true God, who will not give His glory to another in countless variations of "idolatry" and "sorcery."

We read at breakfast the daily chronicle of man's heroic self-assertion, which declares, "My ego is my god—get out of my way, *everybody!*" and documents that devotion to self and defiance of God in works of "enmity, strife, jealousy, anger, selfishness, dissensions, party spirit, envy" at every level—personal, social, and political. The resultant spectacle of everybody trying to shove everybody off the edge of the earth would be comical if the shovers-off were puppets manufactured in the image of man and not men created in the image of God.

The chronicle of man's intoxicated self-assertion has appeared in revised and enlarged editions since Paul's day. The art of chemically distending man's egoistic fantasies has made great strides, and the "flesh" of man has elaborated upon the simple alcoholic "drunkenness" and "carousing" with which man used to declare: "My 'high' is my god: God's stars are but candles to my head."

The battle continues, the war goes on, and even the fleshiest of men realizes in his heart of hearts that it is a battle which he cannot win, a war that he must lose. How then shall the futile struggle be finally resolved, how shall peace be restored? The Law, however wise its measures and however stern its threats, cannot do it; the disrespect into which the slogan "law and order" has fallen of late is a negative witness to the wisdom from on high given to Paul. Paul does not oppose any operation of the Law to the "works of the flesh"; indeed, he sees possibilities of peace only where the sway of the Law has ceased ("You are not under the Law"), only where the Law's prohibition cannot be spoken ("Against such there is no law").

Paul opposes to "the works of the flesh" the "*fruit* of the Spirit." Now "fruit" for Paul is that which grows under the creative blessing of the God who said, "Let light shine out of darkness!" The Creator Spirit, who moved upon the face of the waters at the beginning, brings forth in us that which enables us to "please God," those fruits to which God's law cannot speak its no: "Love, joy, peace, patience, kindness, goodness, faithfulness, gentleness, self-control." For the Spirit gives to us Christ Jesus, or better, He gives us to Christ Jesus; He makes of us "those who belong to Christ Jesus." In Christ we assent to the Law's verdict upon the flesh, and the old war with God is over. By Baptism we have in Christ died the rebel criminal's death of crucifixion; "the flesh with its passions and desires" is dead.

And we are alive, alive to "walk by the Spirit," alive to be "led by the Spirit," alive to do battle when battle must be done (and when victory is sure) against "the desires of the flesh." We fight on the field where Jesus has won the victory, summons us to victory, and equips us for victory with His Spirit. The old man of erotic self-assertion, of religious self-assertion, of heroic self-assertion, of inebriate self-assertion is the already-defeated enemy, and God is on our side:

> Yea, by Thee I can crush a troop,
>   and by my God I can leap over a wall.
> This God—His way is perfect:
>   the promise of the Lord proves true. (2 Sam. 22:30)

The Spirit's Marching Orders

If we live by the Spirit, let us also walk by the Spirit. (Gal. 5:25)

"Live by the Spirit . . . walk by the Spirit." The Greek word translated "walk" has a military ring to it, suggesting a walking in orderly and disciplined ranks. One scholar has attempted to catch this overtone of "walk" with the rendering: "obey the marching orders of the Spirit." With this overtone in mind, we might well say that this sentence of Paul's is a pithy description of all the lives of all the marching sons of God.

It is surely an apt description of the life of the Son of God, Jesus Christ our Lord. His life as the incarnate Son began when His mother Mary "was found to be with child of the Holy Spirit." An angel of the Lord told Joseph, "That which is conceived in her is of the Holy Spirit"; thus the promise made to Mary by the angel Gabriel was fulfilled:

> The Holy Spirit will come upon you,
> and the power of the Most High will overshadow you;
> therefore the Child to be born will be called holy,
> the Son of God. (Luke 1:35)

He lived by the Spirit and He walked by the Spirit. This Israelite, son of Abraham and son of David, did not go the way of the sons of Israel who "rebelled and vexed His [the Lord's] Holy Spirit." He obeyed the marching orders of the Spirit. "Led up by the Spirit," He walked into the wilderness and there spoke the Spirit's no to the devil and the obedient Son's unbroken yes to God. "Full of the Holy Spirit," He walked into the world to meet unwaveringly the world's contradiction and opposition; and when everybody who was anybody in Israel turned from Him, when "the wise and understanding" remained blind to Him and were blinded, when none but the insignificant "babes" accepted Him, when He tasted the cup of failure that was soon to become the cup of suffering and death, He "rejoiced in the Holy Spirit and said, 'Father, I thank Thee!'"

God has predestined us "to be conformed to the image of His Son" and has called us and has given us His Spirit in order that the Son might be "the Firstborn among many brethren." We live by the Spirit; "the law of the Spirit of life in Christ Jesus" has liberated us from the law of sin and death and has given us a life that shall not ever end. As surely as we are sons of God by the Spirit's life-giving work, we are to walk by the Spirit, to obey the marching orders of the Spirit who has enrolled us in the ranks of the army of the sons of God.

That means the end of the self-seeking, self-asserting life of the flesh; that means saying the Son's good-bye to "bread" and to every other attainable and manageable security. That means speaking Jesus' "Father, I thank Thee" in the face of failure and of threatening death. Paul learned to speak that selfless word of thanks in obedience to the Spirit. He was an imprisoned failure when he wrote to the Philippians: "Yes, and I shall rejoice. For I know that through your prayers and the help of the Spirit of Jesus Christ this will turn out for my deliverance, as it is my eager expectation and hope that I shall not be at all ashamed, but that with full courage now as always Christ will be honored in my body, whether by life or by death."

We have begun to hear the Holy Scriptures aright—we have begun to read, mark learn, and inwardly digest them to some purpose—when we have learned to hear them as the marching orders of the Holy Spirit, who gives what He demands and bestows the power to do what He commands. Whether we read the historical records that are Israel's confessions and praise of the inexorable judgment and the indefatigable love of Israel's God, or hear the prayers and praises of the Psalter, or the voices of Israel's prophets recalling Israel from the leaky cisterns of her own digging to the Fountain of living waters in order that Israel may drink and live, or hear Jesus bidding us become what God has made us: sons of the Father in heaven who loves when love has nothing to go on, or listen to Paul as he parses out the Gospel in both the indicative and the imperative mood, or to James as he lays Jesus' call to repentance once more upon our hearts, or to the prophet of Patmos bidding us listen to what the Spirit says to the churches—in all these we hear the marching orders of the Spirit spoken to men on the march toward the city of God, their home. All these voices are the voice of the Spirit, who says: "You are alive —live! You live by My blessing—walk by My power!"

The Promise of Power

I bow my knees before the Father . . . that according to the riches of His glory He may grant you to be strengthened with might through His Spirit in the inner man, and that Christ may dwell in your hearts through faith. (Eph. 3:14, 16-17)

The Third Person of the Holy Trinity tends to come in a poor third. We include Him dutifully enough in our doxology: "Praise Father, Son, and Holy Ghost," but He does not seem ever to bear so concrete, vital, and personal a part in our prayers and praises as the Father and the Son. Perhaps our English usage is partly to blame; what we find in our dictionaries under "spirit" and "spiritual" is but a distant and anemic cousin to what the prophetic and apostolic writings say with those words. If we were to test one another with an instant-association game, who of us would respond to "spirit" with words like "strengthen" and "might"—words that Paul associates so closely with "Spirit"?

And yet power is from the beginning a primary component in the Biblical witness to the Spirit of God. The Spirit was present at creation, when chaos and darkness heard the almighty word of God and took their flight. It was He who empowered the judges, the strong deliverers that God raised up for the deliverance of His people, to do great deeds and win in the face of impossible odds. Samson was but a slippery tool in the hand of the Lord and lost more by his witlessness than he won by his muscle. But when "the Spirit of the Lord came mightily upon him," that power prevailed; "the ropes which were on his arms became as flax that has caught fire, and his bonds melted off his hands," and Samson was free to do the work the Lord would have him do.

But the Spirit enabled men to do greater and more difficult things than killing a thousand Philistines with the jawbone of an ass. The prophet Micah faced down the popular prophets, who told men what they wanted to hear, with the words:

> As for me, I am filled with power,
> with the Spirit of the Lord,
> and with justice and might,
> to declare to Jacob his transgression,
> and to Israel his sin. (Micah 3:8)

The Spirit gave him the power to say, "Thou ailest there and there," and to perform the difficult and dangerous surgery demanded by his people's disease.

"The Spirit of the Lord came mightily upon David" when the prophet Samuel anointed him. In the power of the Spirit he became "the son of Jesse . . . the man who was raised on high." Isaiah saw a new David rise up from "the stump of Jesse," the ruined royal house, and declared concerning great David's greater Son:

> The Spirit of the Lord shall rest upon Him . . .
> the spirit of counsel and might. (Is. 11:2)

When the vision of Isaiah had become history, Peter bore witness to the Son of David in words that recalled the ancient anointed king: "God anointed Jesus of Nazareth with the Holy Spirit and with power." Every record that we have of this Son of David bears witness to His power. Even His opponents could not deny it; they "explained" it without denying it: "He casts out demons by Beelzebub, the prince of demons."

This king, anointed with the Spirit and with power, came to give, not to get after the usual manner of kings. He gave without price all the gifts which proved true the Lord's ancient promise: "I will satisfy the weary soul and every languishing soul I will replenish." He gave of Himself, and He gave Himself, His body and blood. And He gave the Spirit; "Being therefore exalted at the right hand of God, He has poured out this which you see and hear." Thus Peter interpreted the eruption of power which at Pentecost broke down the barriers of language which for centuries had separated man from man.

"You will receive power when the Holy Spirit has come upon you; and you shall be My witnesses" was Jesus' promise to His apostles. The story of the apostles and the apostolic church testifies how sure the promise of Jesus is. And the subsequent history of the church makes clear that Paul's prayer for the church, namely, that the called saints of God "be strengthened with might through His Spirit in the inner man," has been answered. There is a sad and still-continuing record which tells how men have striven to be strengthened with might without the Spirit and without the indwelling of Christ the Crucified in their hearts—how men have changed the church militant into the church military and have reached for the sword which Jesus long ago struck out of His disciple's hand. But there is also the record, often written in tears and blood, of those men genuinely strengthened with might through the Spirit, men in whose heart Christ dwelt by faith, men who learned to speak Jesus' "Thy will be done" and so come to share in His victory.

The church is an anvil that hath worn out many hammers.

Individuality amid Unity

[Be] eager to maintain the unity of the Spirit in the bond of peace. (Eph. 4:3)

"They create a desolation, and they call it peace." That was a Roman historian's comment on the Roman method of pacifying and unifying the Roman Empire. One need not look very hard or very far to find parallels to which the historian's sardonic comment applies. Our human attempts to produce unity and peace all too often purchase unity and peace at the cost of our humanity. Something of our human worth and dignity gets lost; something of what makes human beings precious and beautiful is thwarted or suppressed when we attempt to produce unity and peace. For we must, man being man, almost of necessity impose unity and legislate peace.

"The unity of the Spirit in the bond of peace" is another story. The Spirit does not impose unity and legislate peace; He creates them, and therefore He need not annihilate in order to unite. The Spirit does not simply blank out those impulses of man which pose a threat to unity and peace; His creative breath transfigures them and makes of them what He who created them in man intended them to be — powers for unity and peace. Take those three fertile breeders of dissension and disunity: honor, bread, and sex. What happens when they are touched by the Breath of God?

God intended honor for man and gave him honor. The psalmist standing overawed under the evening sky cries out at it:

> When I look at Thy heavens, the work of Thy fingers,
>   the moon and the stars which Thou hast established;
> what is man that Thou art mindful of him,
>   and the son of man that Thou dost care for him?
> Yet Thou hast made him little less than God,
>   and dost crown him with glory and honor.

It was God, the Lover of variety, who gave to each man an honor peculiarly his own. God made and makes individuals. It was man who made of his honor a caricature of the Creator's intent by declining the honor freely given him by God, who created him in His image, and seeking his own honor in striving to be God's equal. Man corrupted individuality into individualism and made of the peaceful united family of man that God intended into a collection of mad and murderous competitors. But God restored man to honor. Now "we see Jesus," the Man who by the grace of God tasted death for every man, "crowned with glory and honor." Through Him God, still concerned about man's honor, is "bringing many sons to glory." The sun never shone upon a more highly individualized set of sons. We need not fight for individuality or in defense of it; we need not bristle at another's individuality or try to make it look less glorious than our own. The fighting is over; the Spirit gives to each man individually as He wills, and He gives to each for the good of all.

God set man in a garden and gave him the right and the strength to work for his bread, while at the same time God's Son has taught us to ask our Father for our daily bread. Man's rebellious will shut him out from God's garden and set his descendants to fighting one another for bread instead of asking it of a Father who will not give stones when His children cry for bread. The Spirit brings us back into God's family, where all have access to the Father "in one Spirit." In that family there is no squabbling over bread. The Spirit gives the company of those who believe "one heart and one soul," as in the first church in Jerusalem where "no one said that any of the things which he possessed was his own" and all "partook of food with glad and generous hearts." When the Spirit has enriched all with His gifts and is Himself "the guarantee of our inheritance," the transient distinction between rich and poor has lost its power to create disunity and strife.

The Creator implanted in humanity the deep and mysterious lovely impulse that binds man and woman together and sets the solitary in families. There is perhaps no more telling index of the fallenness of fallen man than the ugly countenance that sex has come to wear. The battles waged by male pride and female cunning, the stale contentiousness immortalized in husband-and-wife and mother-in-law jokes, the hot and humid air of intrigue and infidelity, the blight that has fallen on family life — these are not the will of Him who blessed man and woman and bade them be fruitful and multiply. It is we who have made that paradise a paradise lost. But where the Spirit makes man's body His temple and sex is not denied or suppressed but affirmed and hallowed, then there is the possibility of a union between man and woman so profound and so paradisiacally pure that it can serve as the mirror in which we behold the love of Christ for His church and the devotion of the church to her Lord.

The Spirit creates peace and unity in the midst of the disunity of our world. It is not the least of His gifts therefore that He creates in man the will to peace and unity. Rather, He makes us *eager* to maintain the given unity, willing to exert ourselves to tend and foster the exotic plant which grows so precariously on the soil which we have sowed with the thorns and thistles of self-will and strife.

Stamped with the Spirit's Seal

Therefore, putting away falsehood, let everyone speak the truth with his neighbor, for we are members one of another. Be angry but do not sin; do not let the sun go down on your anger, and give no opportunity to the devil. Let the thief no longer steal, but rather let him labor, doing honest work with his hands, so that he may be able to give to those in need. Let no evil talk come out of your mouths, but only such as is good for edifying, as fits the occasion, that it may impart grace to those who hear. And do not grieve the Holy Spirit of God, in whom you were sealed for the day of redemption. Let all bitterness and wrath and anger and clamor be put away from you, with all malice. (Eph. 4:25-31)

"Do not grieve the Holy Spirit." The Spirit is not a vague Force or a general circumambient Atmosphere that somehow influences our lives. The Spirit is God in Person, personally concerned about us. Paul speaks of Him in highly personal terms: the Spirit "sets free," "dwells in" man, "teaches," "bears witness," "helps" (Paul uses the same word that Martha used when she wanted Mary to "lend a hand" with the serving), "cries out" in prayer, "intercedes," "leads," heads a marching troop, "desires," and is "grieved" at the faults and failures of the children of God who do not obey His promptings.

The Spirit who proceeds from the Father and the Son is, like them, not above details and drudgery—like lighting lamps and sweeping out corners in search of one lost coin. The Spirit is ours not only for high "inspired" moments of meditation and worship; He is there to "help us in our weakness" amid our routine and scarcely-noted failures. He notes and is grieved by our little fibs, our convenient falsehoods—those slight bendings of the truth which we deem indispensable for civilized converse with one another.

God's eye is on the sparrow, and He has numbered the hairs of our head. The Spirit is concerned about trifles; for Him it is no little thing when we let the sun go down on our anger, when we go to bed unforgiving and unforgiven, when our "bitterness and wrath and anger and clamor and slander" have given the devil a handhold on men whom God has claimed as His own. He cannot be as casual about our understandable irritations as we think we can be.

The Spirit is grieved when God's uncompromising "Thou shalt not steal" is compromised by men He has condescended to make His dwelling, when we substitute those grayish-gray dark-gray medium-black little means of self-help (which only a hypersensitive conscience would call theft) for the white honesty of hard work and generous giving. The Spirit is grieved when we make a dead letter of the Law which He has inscribed as living oracles upon our hearts. Eyes of the heart enlightened by the Spirit which do not see God's protecting hand held over all that is his neighbor's — eyes which cannot see the difference between "mine" and "thine" — that is a grievous self-contradiction and a contradiction of the Spirit.

The Spirit, who has empowered and impelled us to be the speaking messengers of God's grace and has unsealed our lips to sing His praise, is grieved when "evil talk" comes out of our mouth. He is grieved at our slippery talk, our suggestive humor, our clever skirtings of the edges of indecency. He remembers, when we forget, the words of our Lord: "I tell you, on the Day of Judgment men will render account for every careless word they utter."

The Spirit has good cause to be grieved, for in these little things — our fibs, our frayed tempers, our petty-cash misdemeanors, our slippery stories — the future, the long future, our whole future, is being decided. God's Spirit is God's seal upon us; in bestowing the Spirit He marks us out as His own and puts us under His protection "for the day of redemption." When we grieve the Spirit we break God's seal, deny God's ownership, and forfeit His protection. Then we can no longer look forward to the great Day as Jesus bade us look: "Look up and raise your heads, because your redemption is drawing near"; all that is left us is "a fearful prospect of judgment, and a fury of fire which will consume the adversaries." We dare not presume upon the Spirit and wantonly grieve Him. But sealed with the Spirit, we can depend on Him who intercedes for us and helps us in our weakness to do what we confess of Him: "He daily and richly forgives all sins to me and all believers, and will at the Last Day raise up me and all the dead, and give unto me and all believers in Christ eternal life. This is most certainly true."

Drinking from a Golden Goblet

And do not get drunk with wine, for that is debauchery; but be filled with the Spirit. (Eph. 5:18)

Nature, it is said, abhors a vacuum. This cosmic abhorrence of emptiness has its miniature counterpart in each of us. When God created man He designed for him a filled life. He gave him a home, a mate, a job, and communion with Himself. He gave him a conscious part in His creative work ("Be fruitful and multiply") and in the Creator's dominion ("Fill the earth and subdue it; and have dominion"). When man forfeited his communion with God, futility fell on him and all creation; his life became empty, and he has been haunted ever since by a horror of emptiness.

Try as he will, man cannot fill that emptiness. It was the desire for a fulfilling wisdom that drove man to take and eat forbidden fruit. But the wisdom he found that way was bitter fruit, and all his long quest for wisdom ever since has been a bitter disappointment. The heart of Faust was seared by the one certainty that his accumulated wisdom gave him: "To know that we can know nothing." Omar Khayyam was neither the first nor the last to wail:

> Myself when young did eagerly frequent
> Doctor and Saint, and heard great argument
> About it and about; but evermore
> Came out by the same door where in I went.

Man has tried to fill his emptiness with honor; he has set out on the hard and ruthless road of ambition to achieve fulfillment, to be rid of the abhorred vacuum of futility. But we end up where Alexander ended (who wept because there were no more worlds to conquer) unless a coronary has cut us off before we are old enough or successful enough to weep in lonely eminence.

Man's attempt to fill his emptiness with intoxication has left a record which is a unanimous verdict of condemnation on that attempt. There are no buckets of wine big enough to drown man's desperate emptiness. He may call for madder music and stronger wine until he is blue in the face, but that is all he gets—blue in the face. Not that this has deterred man from trying again and again. He does try again and again. Even the Christian has moments when, worn by the long struggle between the Spirit and the flesh, he is tempted to strike the board and cry, "No more! I will abroad."

> Sure there was wine
> Before my sighs did dry it. There was corn
> Before my tears did drown it.
> Is the year only lost to me?
> Have I no joys to crown it?
> No flowers, no garlands gay? All blasted?
> All wasted?
> Not so, my heart! But there is fruit,
> And thou hast hands.
> Recover all thy sigh-blown age
> On double pleasure.

But then he hears his Lord's voice calling "Child!" and he hears the apostle's voice reminding him that he who goes this way does not achieve a glorious frenzy where he is expansively and poetically happy with vine leaves in his hair, fulfilled and satisfied, that this way ends in bleary-eyed debauchery.

The apostle does not take this cup from our lips without giving us something in its place. Like all God's messengers, he takes from us only in order to give us more than we ourselves have the imagination to dream of or the wit to ask for. He puts a golden goblet to our lips and bids us drink our fill: "Be filled with the Spirit." Here is a wine, here is the only wine, that fills the emptiness of fallen man. On this wine men can sing good songs to man and make grateful melody in their hearts to God. On this wine men are moved to sing together, each man bearing his part, in the heartening harmony of the people of God. On this wine men can grow young again, not for a few fuddled hours but forever; they are renewed to the youthful innocence of man "created after the likeness of God in true righteousness and holiness." Men filled with this wine will not stagger or stray; they walk with steady step in love, in the light, and in wisdom, not in the dry sobriety of cautious prudence but in the clear-eyed wisdom that sees God and knows His will and is glad. This wine is no breaker-up of families nor does it make men forgetful of their duties. Heartened by this wine men can put on the whole armor of God and do victorious battle "against the principalities, against the powers, against the world rulers of this present darkness, against the spiritual hosts of wickedness." The old dark emptiness is gone; man is no longer

> An infant crying in the night,
> An infant crying for the light,
> And with no language but a cry.

Filled with the Spirit, he is a man at last, adult man, complete and fulfilled.

On Wings of Prayer

Pray at all times in the Spirit, with all prayer and supplication. To that end keep alert with all perseverance, making supplication for all the saints, and also for me. (Eph. 6:18-19)

The Spirit and prayer are inseparable. In the Old Testament the prophets, those "men of the Spirit," were from Moses onward men of prayer, intercessors for their people.

In the New Testament Jesus was praying when the Spirit descended upon Him, and the whole life of this Man of the Spirit was a life of prayer, as Luke especially emphasizes in his gospel. When Jesus first sent out the Twelve, He put the key signature of prayer before the music of apostolic ministry: "Pray . . . the Lord of the harvest to send out laborers into His harvest." Paul, the "untimely born" among the apostles, proves himself to be a true apostle of Jesus Christ in this respect also. His letters almost invariably begin with thanksgiving and petition, and he strives to bring his readers into the orbit of his Spirit-filled life of prayer.

According to Paul it is the Spirit who gives us a child's confidence in prayer. For him the fact that we can cry "Abba! Father!" is a sure token of the Spirit's persuasive presence. It is the Spirit who lends wings to our leaden lives that cannot of themselves rise in volatile prayers of hope: "The Spirit helps us in our weakness . . . the Spirit Himself intercedes for us with sighs too deep for words." And it is "in the Spirit" that we are able to pray in that unlikeliest of prayer chapels—the battlefield where we engage the "spiritual hosts of wickedness."

I remember that as a boy I was fond of banging out on the piano a song called *Gebet Waehrend der Schlacht* ("Prayer in the Midst of Battle"). There was in the left hand a soul-satisfying series of sixty-fourth notes designed to imitate the drumfire of artillery, above which the melody of the prayer itself was to soar. The difficulty for me was that the rolling bass notes always threatened to drown out the melody of the prayer. That difficulty is present for us always in our embattled lives of prayer. Perhaps that is why the language of the apostle (who has just been speaking of battle) is so insistent here: "Pray *at all times* . . . with *all* prayer and supplication. . . . *Keep alert* with *all* perseverance, making supplication for all the saints, *and also for me*."

"Pray at all times." There is a constant temptation to put off prayer. In times of crisis we decide to put it off until the more convenient season of calm. In times of calm we defer prayer until a time of crisis shall make prayer imperative. The "spiritual hosts of wickedness" are more clever than we; they know the military value of the perpetual probe and the psychological value of the unexpected sally; they are quick to exploit any opportunity our sloth or carelessness gives them. Therefore Paul's word to us is: "Pray at all times," plug every gap and meet every eventuality with "*all* prayer and supplication."

"Keep alert with all perseverance." We are reminded of the disciple Peter who slept in Gethsemane, forgetting prayer. He rose to futile sword-drawing, to fearful flight and faithless denial. We are reminded, on the other hand, of Jesus' parable of the persevering widow and the unjust judge and His strong word of assurance: "And will not God vindicate His elect, who cry to Him day and night? Will He delay long over them? I tell you, He will vindicate them speedily." God will be faithful, and the Son of Man will be true; we need not worry on that score. We need to worry about ourselves—whether we shall find the heart and the faith to "bother" God, as the widow "bothered" the unjust judge. "When the Son of Man comes, will He find faith upon the earth?"

"Making supplication *for all the saints*." We are not praying "in the Spirit" (who intercedes for the saints) if we pray only for ourselves or, at most, pray us-four-and-no-more prayers:

> Bless me and my wife,
> Son John and his wife;
> Us four,
> And no more.

It was to man's self-seeking will that the Tempter appealed so successfully when our first parents fell. He tried to appeal to the self-seeking will of man again, but unsuccessfully so, when he met Jesus in the wilderness. If we let that self-seeking will invade our prayers, we have already yielded the field to the hosts of wickedness.

"And also for me." Paul has in his Letter to the Ephesians prayed for the church twice, but as a man of the Spirit he cannot let the church be merely the object of his prayers. As surely as he is an apostle of Jesus Christ by the will of God, and as surely as his Christian readers are the apostolic church sealed by the Spirit of God, their intercessions must be mutual. Paul knows: There is no one in the church so weak that he lacks the strength to intercede for others, and there is no one so strong that he can do without the intercession of others. And he knows that we all grow stronger by strengthening one another, for "the whole body . . . *when each part is working properly, makes bodily growth and upbuilds itself in love.*" We sometimes imagine that there are shining souls so strong that they have no need of our intercessions. But we do not know through what dark nights of the soul such men are often led and how much they need and how highly they value the intercessions of us all.

Worship in the Spirit

We are the true circumcision, who worship by the Spirit of God and glory in Christ Jesus. (Phil. 3:3)

If the Spirit is the Spirit of life, He is the Spirit of worship, of praise. The inspired men of the Old Testament teach us that life and praise are inseparably linked. They feel the bitterness of death most keenly in the fact that death means the end of praise:

> The dead do not praise the Lord,
> nor do any that go down into silence. (Ps. 115:17)

When man has ceased to worship, man has ceased to be. It is the peculiar honor of the circumcised, of the people upon whom God has incised His gracious covenant-will, that they are created to be the walking doxology to God. They exist in order to echo and reecho the song of the seraphim until "the whole earth is full of His glory." They are the sons and daughters whom the Lord created for His glory. He is the King of kings, "enthroned on the praises of Israel." When the Lord restores the fortunes of Judah and Israel, when He forgives the guilt of their sin and rebellion against Him, He is recreating the doxology of His people: "This city shall be to Me a name of joy, a praise and a glory before all the nations."

"We are the true circumcision." Jesus has promised that all the ancient distinctions between race and race would disappear and that a new people of God would arise as a people united by a worship in spirit and truth. That promise has been fulfilled. The Father who seeks such worshipers has sought and found us, and Israel's privilege of praise has become ours. We "glory in Christ Jesus" as Israel gloried in the Lord. We have become the light of the world, and our whole life has become a worship that leads men to glorify our Father in heaven. For us now, as for Israel in the past, to live is to praise, and the cessation of doxology is the end of life.

We worship "by the Spirit" as successors and heirs of Israel. We call Abraham our father, we who follow in the footsteps of believing Abraham, and we should prove graceless and forgetful sons if we cut ourselves off from the worship of all earlier sons of Abraham. Our worship has roots in the synagog and the temple, in the faith and worship of Israel. We Gentiles cannot forget Paul's warning directed at Gentile pride: "Remember it is not you that support the root, but the root that supports you." It is not only the perennial attraction of the impassioned poetry of the Psalms that gives them so sure a place in Christian worship, for when the Psalms are sung in the church by "the true circumcision, who worship by the Spirit of God," they are where they belong; only a violent and unnatural divulsion can remove them from thence.

Worship "by the Spirit of God" thus had in it from the beginning a large enrichment from the past. It is natural therefore, if not inevitable, that Christian worship has continued to be "traditional," mindful of all that the past has produced, under the genial breath of the Spirit, in the various tongues and tones of praise. We whose intensest vital impulse it is not to let God's mercies lie

> Forgotten in unthankfulness
> Nor without praises die

dip naturally and joyfully into the treasures of doxology which our fathers have left us.

But neither can we who "worship by the Spirit of God" resignedly believe that the flame of the Spirit has died out or continues to burn but smokily and fitfully in our own day. If we do believe that, it is time for repentance and prayer. And prayer will be heard, and the flame will burn brightly again. We dare not then dream our way back into a comfortable twilit past. That would grieve the Spirit and would quench, so far as in us lies, His flame. Let us believe that the ever-new mercies of God inspire an ever-new song of praise. Let us face the Spirit's new light and spread our numbed hands to warm them at the Spirit's flame, even when the leaping tongues of fire assume strange shapes and the scattering sparks that shoot up our old chimneys pick out new and startling patterns against the velvet soot of the past.

The Spirit
and the Flesh

Beloved, do not believe every spirit, but test the spirits to see whether they are of God; for many false prophets have gone out into the world. By this you know the Spirit of God: every spirit which confesses that Jesus Christ has come in the flesh is of God, and every spirit which does not confess Jesus is not of God. (1 John 4:1-3)

Where God builds churches, the devil builds chapels. The diabolical counterthrust is always an imitation of God's thrust. Where God manifests His fair and truthful works, the devil produces plausible imitations of the true: false prophets, false apostles, false Christs. And such is the diabolic cunning that the false is often more impressive than the true: the false Christ is in his way more splendid and successful than the true Christ, the Servant Christ; the false apostles are more imposing, more eloquent, more brilliant than the true apostles, the servants of Jesus Christ; and the false prophets seem more spiritual than the true prophets, the men of the Spirit of God.

That is what makes the false prophet so dangerous: "Satan disguises himself as an angel of light," and "his servants also disguise themselves as servants of righteousness." John therefore warns his readers against too easy a credulity over against any and everything that marches under the banner of "spirituality." He says, "*Test* the spirits." And he gives them a touchstone wherewith to distinguish between true spirituality and false. That touchstone is Christ's coming "in the flesh," or history. Any proclaimed Christ who is not wholly identifiable with the man Jesus of Nazareth is not the Christ of God, however highly his prophets may exalt him, however loftily they may extol him. The Holy Spirit, the Spirit of God, impels men to confess *Jesus* as Lord and Christ.

How could it be otherwise? The Spirit of God whom we know from the Old Testament has a decided preference for "flesh" and history. He lives and moves and does His work in the world of man, amid the hard realities of history, in time and space. He "clothes Himself" (so the Hebrew Old Testament puts it; English translations soften the expression) with a man like Gideon; He "comes mightily upon" judges and kings and enables them to fight the Lord's battles and win deliverance for the Lord's people by virtue of the power He gives them. Isaiah speaks of the Spirit as *the* power in history, mightier and more decisive than the dreaded and coveted cavalry of Egypt.

"And was incarnate by the Holy Ghost." So our creed sums up the beginning of the story of the Christ. And throughout the continuation of the story of that Spirit-filled and Spirit-led Man has about it the earthy smell of history. The time of His birth and the time of His ministry are synchronized with the reign of Roman emperors and Jewish kings. The Gospels — and the Apostles' Creed after them — have given a dubious kind of immortality to the Roman governor who gave the order for Jesus' execution. Pontius Pilate might have slept peacefully in a footnote in the third volume of a four-volume history of Rome if it were not for the Spirit of God who moved in history and moved men to record that history.

The Gospel according to John has been called "the spiritual Gospel"; and yet, how earthy just that Gospel is! It is John who states the event of the Incarnation most drastically: "The Word became *flesh*." It is John who records the weariness and thirst of the Man beside the well of Jacob in Samaria who begged a drink of a much-married and now nonmarried Samaritan woman. It is John alone who records the "fleshliest" of the words from the cross: "I thirst." And the passion of Jesus — all the evangelists are agreed that this was no shadow play, no spiritual "as-if"; this was blood, sweat, and tears — the story of the Man whose sorry human plight wrung tears from the daughters of Jerusalem.

Why is John so earnestly concerned that we hear the witness of the Holy Spirit which fixes Christ in the flesh and holds us fast in history? We can find the answer readily enough as soon as we envision what we would lose if we substituted a phantom Christ for Jesus Christ come in the flesh.

We lose the Old Testament; we shall have no part in

David, nor in the Son of God "who was descended from David according to the flesh." The Spirit "who spoke by the prophets" may perhaps speak to us in whispers still, but we shall never again hear the full historical ring of His voice as it speaks in the Former Prophets and the Latter Prophets.

We lose Jesus, the compassionate High Priest "who in every respect has been tempted as we are, yet without sinning." And if we can no longer look to Him who "in the days of His flesh offered up prayers and supplications, with loud cries and tears . . . and was heard for His godly fear," how shall we "with confidence draw near to the throne of grace, that we may receive mercy and find grace to help in time of need"?

We lose Jesus the Servant, "who though He was in the form of God . . . emptied Himself, taking the form of a servant, being born in the likeness of men." He "became obedient unto death, even death on a cross." And if we in false spirituality turn from the Son of God turned Servant, how can we hope to join in the cosmic acclamation at the end of days which hails Jesus Christ as Lord to the glory of God the Father?

Uses of the Spirit's Word

All Scripture is inspired by God and profitable for teaching, for reproof, for correction, and for training in righteousness. (2 Tim. 3:16)

We expend a great many adjectives in our attempts to convey the overwhelming effect that the Scriptures have on us. Paul uses only two: "inspired" and "profitable." "Inspired"—the creative power of the Spirit produced the Scriptures; "men moved by the Holy Spirit spoke from

God." The power of the Spirit produced the Holy Scriptures, and the power of the Spirit is at work in them.

That is what makes them "profitable," useful, "able to instruct . . . for salvation through faith in Christ Jesus." The Spirit's Word has the power to give us freely and abundantly what we cannot give ourselves. His Word is useful "for teaching," for the one teaching that matters supremely, the teaching of God. Left to ourselves, we shall but stray, for we construct gods in our own image and create a creator who is the answer to our desires. The Spirit's Word puts us into the presence of God Himself, the God of immeasurable power before whom the nations are like drops from a bucket, and all the prancing majesties of man are "accounted as dust on the scales"; the God of immeasurable wisdom who destroys the wisdom of the wise and thwarts the cleverness of the clever; the God of immeasurable goodness who in the midst of wrath remembers mercy, who will not execute His fierce, deserved anger and will not come to destroy because He is God and not man, "the Holy One in your midst," "who did not spare His own Son but gave Him up for us all."

The Spirit's Word is useful "for reproof." "Reproof" is a bit weak to convey the force of the original here. The idea is not merely that the Word reproves us but rather that it *convicts* us. Brought by the Spirit's power into the presence of God, we realize what God really is—and what we really are. We are moved to say what Isaiah once said when he saw the Lord sitting upon a throne, high and lifted up, and heard the seraphim calling to one another, "Holy, holy, holy is the Lord of hosts"—we are moved to repeat Isaiah's cry: "Woe is me! For I am lost; for I am a man of unclean lips, and I dwell in the midst of a people of unclean lips." We are convicted of our unholiness by the very presence of the Holy One of Israel.

The story of the vision of Isaiah does not end with his hopeless cry or with his "conviction." A seraph takes a burning coal from the Lord's altar and with it touches the prophet's unclean lips. Thus the prophet, touched with hallowed fire, is permitted to hear the absolution which is God's "correction" of guilty man: "Behold, this has touched your lips; your guilt is taken away, and your sin forgiven." "Reproof" is not the last word for us either, for we hear the inspired Word which sets us, all unholy as we are, in the presence of the holy God. The Spirit of wisdom and revelation gives us the eyes of an heart enlightened to behold the "correction" by which God raises up fallen man and the fallen world; He gives us eyes to behold the Lord Jesus Christ, a mouth to confess Him as Lord — and hearts to believe that God has raised Him from the dead.

When we have thus seen Him, confessed Him, and believed in Him we are ready for the next stage of the Spirit's profitable work; we are ready for "training in righteousness." We have heard the invitation of Him who knows the Father and has chosen to reveal the Father to us. In our hopeless weariness under the yoke of the law we have heard Him say, "Come to Me . . . and I will give you rest," and we are ready to receive the easy yoke of Him who has borne our burdens for us.

Teaching, reproof, correction, training in righteousness — these are the gifts which the Spirit offers us in His Word. To the end that these gifts may be ours, we pray that we may "hear . . . read, mark, learn, and inwardly digest" the Holy Scriptures written for our learning. These are gifts of infinite value, worth every expenditure of brains and energy needed to receive them. For these gifts we should be ready to give up that easy Christian indolence which conceals its sloth with the wrappings of piety and takes comfort in the conviction that the use of the human intellect is incompatible with the activity of the Spirit.

We might do the Spirit the honor to believe that He knows best what gifts we need. We do violence to the Scriptures and dishonor to the Spirit when we seek to extract from the Scriptures all manner of curious lore which they were never designed to yield, when we refuse to leave unanswered all manner of peripheral questions which the Spirit has not deigned to answer. And we might consider also that perhaps the Giver of the gifts knows best how to wrap His gifts. It is a shabby sort of appreciation that will attempt to rewrap them, for example, by turning His substantial poetry into prose and His plain-spoken prose into insubstantial poetry.

Our Guide into All Truth

Immediately the father of the child cried out and said, "I believe; help my unbelief!" (Mark 9:24)

When Jesus came down from the calm glory of the mount of transfiguration, the misery of man swept around Him once more. There pressed upon Him the agony of the boy possessed of an evil spirit that convulsed him and sought to destroy him, and the despair of the boy's father who had sought help from Jesus' disciples in vain. It was the unbelief which showed itself in the father's despair and in the disciples' inability to help that touched Jesus most painfully and wrung from Him the cry: "O faithless generation, how long am I able to be with you? How long am I to bear with you?" And when the father addressed his plea to Jesus Himself with halfhearted diffidence ("*If you can do anything,* have pity on us and help us"), Jesus, the Pioneer of all human faith, turned on him with words born of His unwavering trust in God the Helper: "If you can! All things are possible to him who believes." To this the father replied with the prayer that all of us have said after him time and time again: "I believe; help my unbelief!" The appeal to Jesus' pity was not made in vain; no such appeal was ever made in vain. Jesus rebuked the unclean spirit and restored the demon-racked boy to humanity. "Jesus took him by the hand and lifted him up, and he arose."

That was Jesus' answer then to the man who wanted to believe but found it impossible to believe. What is His answer now to us for whom faith and unbelief lie in dubious conflict joined? How does the exalted Lord respond when one of us cries, "I believe; help my unbelief"? (We thank God for a Lord to whom we may cry thus out of the depths.) The response of our Lord is the sending of the Counselor, the Spirit of truth. "I tell you the truth," Jesus told His disciples when their hearts were filled with sorrow at the thought of His departure, "it is to your advantage that I go away, for if I do not go away, the Counselor will not come to you; but if I go, I will send Him to you."

> Alleluia! not as orphans
> Are we left in sorrow now.
> Alleluia! He is with us . . . .

He is with us indeed, for the Spirit of truth does, as Jesus has promised, teach us all things and does bring to remembrance all that the incarnate Word has spoken. He bears witness to Jesus so persuasively and powerfully that we are able to bear witness too. He guides us into all truth and brings home to us all the compassionate and gracious glory wherewith the Father has glorified the Son. As has been well said, the work of the Spirit is not so much to supply Jesus' absence as to complete His presence.

He is with us, and He wills to be found by us, if we will but seek Him where He is to be found: in Baptism, "the washing of regeneration and renewal in the Holy Spirit"; in His Supper, where we are all made to drink of one Spirit"; in the Word of His witnesses who speak to us in accents "not taught by human wisdom but taught by the Spirit"; in the Word of the goodly fellowship of the prophets who unite to bear witness to Him. He is with us, eternally marked as the Compassionate by those

> Rich wounds yet visible above
> In beauty glorified.

We can still appeal to that compassion, as the desperate father once did: "Have pity on us and help us." And so limitless is His compassion that, helped by the Spirit in our weakness, we dare to pray: "I believe, help my unbelief!"

Waiting for the Bridegroom

The Spirit and the bride say, "Come." And let him who hears say, "Come." (Rev. 22:17)

In the Revelation to John the bride signifies the church, "the holy city . . . prepared as a bride adorned for her husband." The adornment of the bride is the Spirit given by God to dwell in the church. And so the Spirit's cry is also, naturally, the cry of the bride: "Come, Lord Jesus!" Naturally, for the Spirit is the beginning and guarantee of our inheritance of the world to come. When the Spirit is at work in Baptism, we there cross the frontier from the region and shadow of death into God's land of eternal light and life. Where He bestows the gift of our Lord's presence in the Lord's Supper, there we have a foretaste of the glad hour of our reunion with Him in the kingdom of His Father, seated at His generous table and drinking with Him the new wine of the ultimate Passover. Where the Spirit lets us hear the voice of the Good Shepherd who died for us and rose again, there we are safely at home with the Good Shepherd forever.

As the Spirit is the beginning and guarantee of our future, so it is not the least of His blessings that He creates in us the homesickness for our everlasting home which is the characteristic token of the church as the waiting bride of Christ. When we are so overwhelmed by sorrow, so muted by melancholy, so oppressed by anxiety and all the fuss and fretting of our daily lives that we lose sight of—and lack the heart to pray for—the world to come, "the Spirit helps us in our weakness"; He "intercedes for us according to the will of God," and we can pray: "Thy kingdom come" with a will once more.

When we become so drunk with the beauty and satisfactions of this world, entrancing even now, however dimmed and distorted its primordial beauty may be by the havoc wrought by man's disobedience; when we become so absorbed in the machinery of those good institutions (the state, the operation of law, the solid structures of decency and beneficence) by which God shores up our ramparts against the encroaching powers of chaos; when we are so interested in life now that we forget how God's clockwork works steadily, though incalculably, toward the dawning of His Day of Judgment and renewal and the life of the world to come; when we forget the new heavens and the new earth where righteousness shall have its sure and settled abode, a world no longer threatened by demonic powers of revolt; when the melody of our lives threatens to become a circular jingle which drowns out God's meaningful melody moving toward its final cadence and triumphant close; when we begin to pray, "Give us our annually guaranteed cake" instead of "Give us this day our daily bread"—then the Spirit lets us hear once more the haunting melody of our homeland, lets us scent the morning air of God's Day, lets us see the lineaments of Him "who gave Himself for our sins to deliver us from the present evil age," and lets us be the church again, the Bride of Christ, singing the song of the Spirit and the bride, "Our Lord, come!" Maranatha!